Alan Hankinson was born in 1926 and educated at Bolton School and Magdalen College, Oxford. He worked for many years as a journalist on the Bolton Evening News, with the Nigerian Broadcasting Corporation as News Editor, and with the Independent Television News in London.

He has done much climbing, especially in the Lake District and North Wales, with occasional forays to the Alps and two expeditions to the Himalayas (Annapurna 1970 and Changabang 1974).

Since 1975 he has been a freelance writer and journalist, living in the Lake District. His previous books include:

The First Tigers (Dent, 1972 & Mara Books, 2005)

Changabang (Heinemann, 1975)

Camera on the Crags (Heinemann, 1975)

Geoffrey Winthrop Young (Hodder and Stoughton, 1995)

Climbers on the Parson's Nose, Crib-y-Ddysgl

The Mountain Men

A history of early Rock Climbing in North Wales –
from its beginning to 1914

ALAN HANKINSON

MARA BOOKS

First published by **Heinemann Educational Books Ltd**. 1977

This edition published in 2004 by **Mara Books**, 22 Crosland Terrace, Helsby, Frodsham, Cheshire WA6 9LY.

ISBN 1 902512 11 1

To 'Len' with gratitude and affection.

Design and additional photography by Carl Rogers.
Printed and bound in Great Britain by Cromwell Press.

The Photographs of the Abraham Brothers appear by courtesy of the
Fell and Rock Climbing Club.

CONTENTS

ACKNOWLEDGEMENTS

MY thanks are due to many: to the distinguishecd mountaineers named in the source notes who gave me information either by interview or by letter; to Mr Edward Pyatt who lent me his unpublished work on O. G. Jones; to the staff of the County Archivist in Caernarfon; to Mrs Muriel Files for access to the library of the Fell and Rock Climbing Club; and to successive librarians at the Alpine Club in London. Mr Chris Briggs of the Pen-y-Gwryd Hotel let me peruse the visitors' books there and the 'Locked Book'. Mr. Harold Drasdo let me borrow the Pen-y-Pass book and also drew the Lliwedd routes on plate 8. Mr Harvey Lloyd of the Pen-y-Pass Youth Hostel went to considerable trouble to find some elusive photographs. Mr. Geoffrey Trevelyan allowed the use of two pictures of Geoffrey Young. Mr. Ken Wilson helped with the picture research. I am grateful to the Fell and Rock Climbing Club for permission to use the photographs of the Abraham brothers.

The lines of verse that introduce each chapter are taken from the poems of Geoffrey Young. The more up-to-date information about Snowdonia climbing comes, chiefly, from the series of guidebooks published by the Climbers' Club.

Finally, three areas of more personal indebtedness: to Mr. Chris Faulds, climber and cameraman, who accompanied me up some of the easier routes mentioned in this book; to my wife, who did the typing and kept a closely-scrutinising eye on both style and content; and to 'Len', Mrs Eleanor Winthrop Young, widow of the central figure in this story. Without her unfailing and buoyant help, in long conversations and much correspondence, in suggesting contacts and finding references, above all in transcribing passages from her late husband's personal diaries, it would hardly have been possible to write the book at all.

GLOSSARY

abseil, descending by sliding down a fixed rope

a cheval, sitting astride a narrow ridge to work your way along it

alpenstock, long wooden pole with a spike at the end

arête, a sharp, narrow ridge

artificial climbing, climbing with the aid of pitons, étrier, etc.

belay (verb), the act of a stationary climber securing himself by fixing the rope round some stable rock projection; (noun) the pro jection itself.

bouldering, practice-climbing on boulders where extreme difficulties can be tackled because there is little distance to fall

col, a mountain pass; the lowest point in a ridge that connects two peaks.

cornice, overhanging lip of snow along a ridge.

crampon, steep-spiked frames, fitted to boots for climbing ice or hard snow; sometimes called 'claws'.

crux, the hardest move, or moves, on a climb.

étrier, short rope-ladder used in modern artificial climbing to surmount holdless or overhanging rock

girdle traverse, roughly horizontal route across a cliff or face from one side to the other.

karabiner, oval-shaped metal link with a spring-hinged gate; sometimes called 'snap-link'.

leading through, fast method by which two roped climbers alternate the lead

pitch, section of a climb between ledges or belay points

piton, metal spike which is hammered into cracks to make belays more secure

scarpetti, light, rope-soled boots.

slings, loops of rope or tape, used for belaying.

top rope, rope secured from above the climber.

traverse, to climb across, rather than up, a cliff.

tricouni, hard steel boot nail with serrated edge.

MAP OF THE SNOWDON AREA

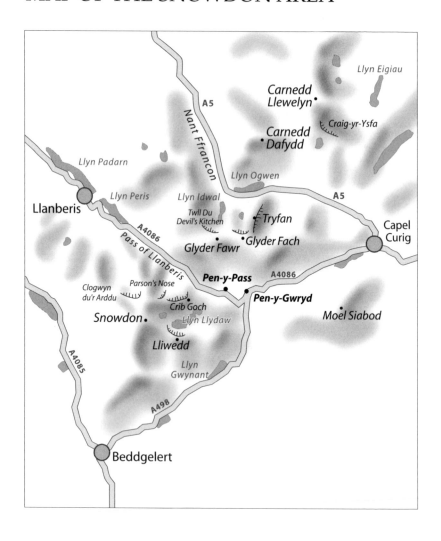

LIST OF PLATES

Chapter I

'THE ROMANTIC TRUST'

Only a hill; but all of life to me,
up there, between the sunset and the sea.

ROCK climbing in North Wales was the creation of a small group of men who shared three qualities: a zest for the sport, a high level of culture and education, and a uniquely romantic attitude. In the few years before the First World War they formed a remarkable holiday community whose memory can still be evoked by the phrase 'the Pen-y-Pass parties'. Their climbing achievement was considerable. But their special significance lay not so much in what they did as in the way they thought and felt about it, and their particular and distinctive attitude to the sport.

Their spirit was reflected again and again in their writings. Hugh Rose Pope, describing the solitary climber, said: 'He is alone with the hills, and stands like one initiated into a strange and beautiful mystery.' C. D. Robertson wrote: 'For some of us at least the most potent spell is not danger, nor beauty, nor fulness of life, but a simple call, a sense of craving when we are not with the mountains, of content when they stand about us.' And in a long article George Mallory strove to discover what it was that distinguished 'those who take a high line about climbing':

Climbing for them means something more than a common amusement, and more than other forms of athletic pursuit mean to other men; it has a recognised importance in life. If you could deprive them of it they would be conscious of a definite degradation, a loss of virtue. . . . . A day well spent in the Alps is like some great symphony. . . . . The spirit goes on a journey just as does the body. . . . The individual is in a sense submerged, yet not so as to be less conscious; rather his consciousness is specially alert, and he comes to a finer realisation of himself than ever before. It is these moments of supremely harmonious experience that remain always with us and part of us.

To some climbers at the time and to countless climbers since, this way of approaching the sport has seemed ridiculously high-flown and presumptuous. It is doubtful whether any modern mountaineer would write in such terms and unlikely that any editor would publish it if he did. But Mallory was speaking not just for himself but for the majority of his mountain companions. The spirit he proclaimed was the special spirit that infused the pioneer climbers in Snowdonia and gave a unique and unmistakable tone to their period. They were self-aware men and self-analytical, sometimes subtle and usually complicated in character, yet there was a fresh and almost boyish idealism about them. Never again, after their work, would the cliffs of North Wales lie so open to the explorer. Never again, after the cruel interruption of the First World War, would the sport be pursued in quite the same buoyant and romantic frame of mind.

The definitive statement of their attitude was made a century before their time, by William Wordsworth in his *Lines Composed a Few Miles above Tintern Abby*:

> . . . . And I have felt
> A presence that disturbs me with the joy
> Of elevated thoughts; a sense sublime
> Of something far more deeply interfused,
> Whose dwelling is the light of setting suns,
> And the round ocean and the living air,
> And the blue sky, and in the mind of man:
> A motion and a spirit, that impels
> All thinking things, all objects of all thought,
> And rolls through all things. Therefore am I still

A lover of the meadows and the woods,
And mountains. . . .

Oddly enough, the 'Lakeland' approach to nature and mountains had little influence on the first generation of British rock climbers. In the 1880s and 1890s the sport of rock climbing—as distinct from high mountaineering which had been practised in the Alps since the middle years of the century—was born and sturdily bred in the Lake District on the cliffs around Wasdale Head. Around the leading figures, Walter Parry Haskett Smith and later Owen Glynne Jones, there grew up a cheerful climbing community, devoted to vigorous expeditions from the Wastwater Hotel. But for them climbing was never more than a holiday pastime. They enjoyed the companionship and the heightened sensations of struggle and uncertainty and conquest that came from finding new and increasingly difficult routes. Their achievements, in purely climbing terms, were more impressive than those of their Snowdonia successors. But their attitude to the sport was practical and physical. They saw the crags as a stimulating challenge to nerve and muscle, not as a source of spiritual inspiration. Their writings abound with such phrases as 'it was a pretty little rock problem'; 'a veritable rock gymnasium'; 'we had a rare little fight . . . and voted it a piece of solid good business'. There was a straightforward, adventurous, almost swashbuckling spirit about them, but little or nothing of the Wordsworthian sense of communion and self-exploration. They did not theorize about the sport or try to analyse their motives or probe into their deeper responses.

It is possible to make too much of the contrast between the first two generations of British rock climbers, the Cumbrian and the Cambrian pioneers. No doubt there were Lake District men who were touched by the romantic spirit, though there were none who expressed it with any force. There must also have been Snowdonia men who took the practical, down-to-earth approach and had little time for high-flown poetic fancies. There was certainly a good deal of intermingling and overlapping between the two groups and many men climbed with equal cheerfulness in both regions. Yet it remains true that the Snowdonia pioneers were, on the whole, more elevated in their approach to the sport than their Lakeland counterparts, more intellectually probing and more spiritually aware.

One reason for this may lie in the nature of the terrain itself. Snowdonia is more extensive than the Lake District, with higher mountains and bigger, darker cliffs and bleaker valleys—a place where a man might feel more removed from his everyday preoccupations and closer to the eternal. The Lake District is altogether more gentle and welcoming, greener and more varied in aspect, more humanly manageable in feeling.

Another reason may be found in the changing spirit of the time, The Lakeland school was founded and flourished in the last two decades of Queen Victoria's reign when the British were able to enjoy the confidence that came from knowing they were supreme in industrial production, in naval might, and in the extent of their imperial power. The Snowdonia school, however, was taking over the path-finding role in the sport at the time when a new monarch, Edward VII, assumed the throne and a new spirit was beginning to make itself felt. Although the Edwardian era has often been portrayed as a kind of Indian summer of British greatness, it did not particularly feel like that to the people at the time. The Boer War had been a shattering and disuniting experience. The armaments race with Germany was gathering momentum and Britain's industrial and commercial supremacy were coming under challenge from the same source. More than that, there were mounting rumblings, of discontent at home—from the working classes, from women militants, and in Ireland. Among thinking men it was a time for doubt. The old Victorian certainties—belief in continuous progress towards Utopia, in the beneficence of the capitalist economy, in Kiplingesque jingoism—no longer seemed so certain. Many of the educated men of Edwardian England, especially the younger men, were looking for nobler causes. Some of them developed an almost mystical sense of man's purpose and destiny. All too soon it was to lead them into the murderous mud of Flanders with the words of Rupert Brooke ringing in their ears.

But this was nothing more than a conditioning factor. The fundamental reason why the first generation of rock climbers in North Wales adopted their special and distinctive tone is clear enough and much closer at hand. It lies in the characters of the twin heroes of this story, James Merriman Archer Thomson and Geoffrey Winthrop Young.

They were both men of culture and concerned with education, and they both enjoyed climbing for the same basic motive. These things apart, however, they could hardly have been more contrasting in character. Archer Thomson, the senior by thirteen years, was an intensely introverted man, withdrawn and moody, a man of pathological reserve. Geoffrey Young, on the other hand, although he was deeply self-aware, was highly sociable and fluently articulate in conversation and in print. The one presented to the world a silent and forbidding front while the other devoted his life to cherishing and sharing his enthusiasms, pouring out a generous stream of affection and instruction and self-expression. These were the men who created rock climbing in North Wales and set its initial tone. And they were both deeply imbued with the romantic spirit.

With Archer Thomson, of course, it was rarely allowed to show. He spoke sparingly and guardedly and when he was persuaded to write about climbing he was usually careful to cloak his feelings in factual description and pedagogic humour. Only very occasionally did he permit something of his inner self to gleam through. He once wrote, for example: 'The kindred pursuits, of rock climbing in Britain and of mountaineering in the Alps have a common origin in a love of mountains, a taste for romance, and a sensibility to the subtle charms of exploration.' And Geoffrey Young said of him: 'He regarded his relations with the hills, and with what they yielded him of success, as a romantic trust.'

Young took precisely the same view and throughout a long and busy life in mountaineering, through his talk and his prose and his poems, his message remained constant:

> To the true mountaineer the 'precious things of the lasting hills' are a trust . . . in return for my guardianship of their integrity they offer me a sanctuary for all the higher impulses, all the less sordid hopes and imaginings which visited me anywhere through the years. Whatever of honourable purpose or of unselfish delight the way of

life suggested, I had but to put it to the test of a mountain setting and share it, when proven, with the heights and the wind, and I could be certain of finding it again, untouched by time and reinvigorating as youth itself, whenever and wherever I returned among the hills. Solitude was essential for the creation of this mutual understanding with the mountains.

And in one of his later poems he wrote:

> If I could seal a hope for younger time,
> climbers to come, then it should be for you
> to know of only two
> verities, yourself and the hill you climb:
> only two voices, the mountain's and your own.

It was Archer Thomson who initiated the exploration of Snowdonia's cliffs and who continued for many years to be the leading innovator on the rock. He was the better rock climber perhaps, but Young was the better all-round mountaineer. And it was Young who gathered around himself a glittering group of friends, created the community and inspired its special spirit.

Their chief meeting places were two hotels at the eastern end of the Llanberis Pass. During the first years the Pen-y-Gwryd Hotel was the focal point and it was from there that the Climbers' Club was formed. Later they moved a mile or so up the hill to Pen-y-Pass, closer to the cliffs of the Snowdon range where their chief interest lay, and here they formed the tradition of the Pen-y-Pass parties.

For a few years up to 1914 Geoffrey Young virtually commandeered the hotel for the Christmas and Easter holidays and filled it with his friends, mostly men but some women and children as well. They climbed vigorously and inventively during the day and enjoyed themselves equally vigorously in the evenings, with songs and games and conversation. An informal body of customs and observances and in-jokes grew up around them. They were not exclusive—every holiday brought some new faces—and if they came almost exclusively from the same social class, it was because in those days the sport was only available and attractive to professional and highly educated men.

Within that limitation they were a varied company. The predominant professions were teaching and the law. Archer Thomson was a headmaster, O. G. Jones and George Mallory were schoolmasters, and Geoffrey Young taught at Eton for a while and then became one of His Majesty's Inspectors of Schools. The lawyers tended to be solicitors and a surprising number of them came from Merseyside. But other professions were well represented too, architects and engineers, scientists and university dons and civil servants, many of them already eminent in their fields. Younger recruits were drawn in mainly from the public schools and the old universities, and several of them, those who were spared by the War, were to become widely famous—Julian Huxley the biologist, for example, and his polymath brother Aldous; Duncan Grant the artist and Robert Graves the writer.

Cambridge produced more recruits than Oxford, but no single college was more consistently represented than Magdalen College, Oxford, with A. W. Andrews, A. D. Godley the classics don, and the botanist Professor Bretland Farmer.

Their numbers were further swelled by a regular contingent from Ireland and a scattering of Alpine veterans and the occasional visiting Alpine guide. Most of them were members of the Alpine Club as well as the Climbers' Club and spent their summer holidays in the mountains of Switzerland and France and Northern Italy. The great majority were English. In contrast with the Lake District school, they were not joined by any of the local hill people. The few Welshmen among them, Humphrey Jones and Siegfried Herford for example, were not mountain men by either origin or background.

The effective period of their activity on the crags spanned twenty years. In the autumn of 1894, when Archer Thomson first formed the habit of walking up to the high valleys every week-end to climb with one or two friends, the great cliffs of Snowdonia were virtually unknown. By the autumn of 1914 there were more than thirty climbers' routes on Lliwedd alone, and over a hundred on the other crags, some of them still graded 'Severe'. Lliwedd was their continuing favourite but they climbed frequently on other cliffs of the Snowdon massif, on Tryfan and the Glyders, in the Carnedds and on many subsidiary hills.

They found previously unsuspected climbing grounds on Craig yr Ysfa, Creigiau Gleision and among the mountains beyond Llyn Cwellyn. They introduced women to the new sport, so that it was natural and appropriate that the first new rock route ever made by a woman should be in Snowdonia. They discovered and developed the 'girdle traverse', the art of picking a way more or less horizontally across a cliff face.

They left severely alone some of the cliffs that have fascinated later generations of climbers, Clogwyn du'r Arddu, for example, and the abrupt outcrops on the northern flank of the Llanberis valley. No doubt the steepness of these crags and the absence of obvious lines of weakness—the first routes were generally gully climbs—made them seem too forbidding. There was, anyway, generous scope for exploration elsewhere. And the pioneers had none of the special equipment and techniques for protecting the leader on a long run-out of the rope—pitons and karabiners, nuts and slings—which their successors were able to use so effectively. They had a rope and nailed boots and that was all.

Their achievement was greater than their climbing alone. Through the Climbers' Club they made the first attempt to bring together rock climbers from all parts of the country and the initial, tentative moves towards a national organization for the sport. They produced the first pocket guide, books to climbing routes on the home cliffs and set the pattern for all subsequent work in this field. They broke new ground in trying to analyse and codify the requirements of the sport and in applying genuine literary talents to the task of describing what it felt like to be on the virgin rock faces of Britain. They brought a generation of fresh recruits to the young sport. And among their ranks they numbered men like Archer Thomson and Siegfried Herford whose names are writ large in the history of British rock climbing; others, Geoffrey Young in particular, who extended the horizons of Alpine mountaineering; and one man, George Mallory, who will be remembered for as long as men remember Mount Everest itself.

The great period of the Pen-y-Pass parties was short. But it was happy and vital and creative, and the special delight of that time was increased, in a way, by a sense that it could not last long and would never be recaptured. Something of what it must have felt like to be part of the community is evoked by passages from Geoffrey Young's personal diary, never intended for publication:

> Easter Vac., 1909. Alone with, Mallory for a week. . . . At first bitter blizzard, and driven off Parson's Nose. Then perfect weather. Explored Craig yr Ysfa . . . three new climbs, bathing each time on way back. Then did Mallory's Slab climb on Lliwedd East Buttress. The hardest rocks I have done yet. . . .
>
> Easter, 1910. Page Dickinson spoke of the feeling of brotherhood which 'was like being in heaven'. Surely we *are* a wonderful brotherhood.
>
> 1911, Easter Vac. Huge and gay party at Pen-y-Pass. Hotel and shacks full and two cottages. . . . Climbed much. . . . Great and unforgettable party in every way, great singing and fun and lovely letters later about it all. . . .
>
> Christmas, 1911. At Pen-y-Pass. The most glorious of all parties. . . My new contingent from Oxford. . . . Mallory again. . . Some great climbing. Gorgeous music at nights.
>
> Christmas Day on Tryfan. We all knew such a time could hardly repeat.

The name of the game was rock climbing and they were devoted to it. But there was more to it than that. They respected courage and skill on the crags but the most important thing to them was the spirit in which a man climbed. They sought not just the companionship of the rope but social companionship in the evenings and the intellectual exhilaration that comes from encountering keen and clear-minded argument. They liked to find new routes on the cliffs where no man had been before. But they also enjoyed re-climbing old routes, sometimes in company, often alone. Fundamentally, the route they were seeking was the one that would take them closer to their own souls.

Chapter II

SNOWDONIA: MYTH AND HISTORY

Look back a thousand years, a thousand more,
There were boys afoot by Llydau's shore. . . .

THE high points of the Snowdonia mountains vary between 2.500 feet above sea level and Y Wyddfa, the summit of Snowdon itself, at 3,560. There are straightforward walkers' ways to all of them which have been known to local shepherds for many centuries. But they are high and inhospitable enough to have kept at bay all curious visitors until comparatively recent times. Until the sixteenth century the only men, apart from the shepherds, who ventured into and above the high valleys did so because they were fugitives, some historical, some legendary.

Llywelyn ap Griffith, for example, took refuge there in the early years of the thirteenth century, and two centuries later the fiery Owen Glendower sought sanctuary in the mountains from the armies of Henry IV. And long before them, according to myth, the mountains were host to King Arthur himself.

Scholars now believe that there probably was an historic original for the legendary king, a Romanized Briton called Ambrosius Aurelianus who lived in the turbulent times just after the Romans had left Britain and who led a small but dedicated force of cavalry in a gallant campaign against the invading Saxons. The writers of the Middle Ages wove many wonderful stories around his name, and the Welsh story-tellers incorporated him into their own legends. According to one of them, Arthur came to Snowdonia to rid it of the pestilential attentions of an ogre called Rhita Gawr. Another tale says that Arthur and his men fought their last battle on Bwlch Y Saethau, the 'Pass of the Arrows', the main gap in the ridge between the summits of Snowdon and Lliwedd. They were defeated and the king was killed and buried there at a spot called Carnedd Arthur. His men then retreated to Lliwedd and climbed down the cliff to a large cave, Ogof Lanciau Eryri—the cave of the Youth of Snowdonia—to sleep there until Arthur, the once and future king, should come again to lead them in battle.

The cave is said to be in the Slanting Gully and a much later Welsh legend, recorded in 1899, tells of a rock climbing shepherd who saw a light in the cave entrance and was rash enough to investigate. As he was squeezing in he banged his head on a great bell, awoke the warriors from their long hibernation and their belligerent shouts—presumably they thought they were off to battle again—gave him a shock from which he never recovered.

The Snowdonia hills are 'old in story' and venerable in history too. Many of the names we use today are at least a thousand years old. A charter of 1198, a grant of lands to the Abbey of Aberconwy, mentions several places, among them Grybgoch (Crib Goch), Chwmdelif (Cwm Dyli) and Wedduavaur (Y Wyddfa). Ninety years later, the Welsh cleric, Giraldus Cambrensis, showed that Snowdon had already acquired its modern place-names. He made a tour of Wales and wrote a topographical description, *Itinerarium Cambriae*, in which he said: 'I must not pass over in silence the mountains called by the Welsh Eryri, but by the British Snowdon, or Mountains of Snow, which . . . seem to rear their lofty summits even to the clouds.' The Welsh name is generally taken to mean 'the abode of eagles' though some scholars interpret it simply as 'the high land'.

For centuries after this, however, the barren nature of the mountains and their savage weather and possibly, also, the fact that such few inhabitants as there were spoke no English, made for a seclusion that was virtually total. There were no coach roads into Snowdonia, there were no books about it, there were no reliable maps. It was not until the Tudor period, when interest began to stir in many branches of learning and exploration, that the region started to receive attention.

Between 1536 and 1539 John Leland, a scholar from Cambridge who had become Henry Vlll's Library Keeper and Antiquary, travelled extensively in Wales. His chief aim was to list items of antiquarian value that had survived the dissolution of the monasteries, and his references to the mountains are scant and dismissive. 'Caernarvonshire,' he says, 'about the shore hath reasonable good corne. . . Then more upwards be Eryry Hilles and in them ys very little corne, except otes in sum places, and a little barle, but scantly rye.' He describes the valleys as thickly wooded and rich in deer, and Snowdon itself as 'horrible with the sights of bare stones'. He was dismissive, too, of the Welsh people. The gentry were men of 'but mean estate', and the common folk 'dyd study more to Pasturage than Tylling, as Favourers of Their consuete idleness'.

Half a century later, the Oxford antiquary William Camden published, in Latin, a geographical account of Britain which was to prove influential. He travelled the formidable coastal route north from Bangor:

> From hence the shore with a steep ascent passes by a very high and perpendicular rock called Penmaenmawr: which hanging over the sea, affords travellers but a very narrow passage; where the rocks on the one hand seem ready to fall on their heads; and on the other, the roaring sea of a vast depth.

For all his academic eminence, Camden propagated some strange misconceptions. Speaking of Caernarvonshire, he says: 'On the interior parts nature has reared groups of mountains as if she meant here to bind the island fast to the bowels of the earth'—mountains seen as nature's nails. And the notion that Snowdon holds snow throughout the year derived from Camden and was reinforced by the Jacobean map-maker John Speed who drew Snowdon on his map twice the height and bulk of the surrounding hills and wrote in his accompanying note:

> These mountains may not unfitly be termed the British Alpes, as being the most vaste of all Britaine, and for their steepnesse and

cragginesse not unlike to those of Italy, all of them towering up into the Aire, and round encompassing one farre higher than all the rest, peculiarly called Snowdon-Hill. . . . For all the yeare long these lye mantelled over with Snow hard crusted together, though otherwise for their height they are open and liable both to the Sunne to dissolve them, and the winds to over-sweepe them.

All the curious visitors so far had been content to make their observations from the valleys and leave the mountaineering to the locals. So the visit of Thomas Johnson has a special significance, in fact a double significance, for he made the first recorded ascent of Snowdon and his motive was one that was to play a formative part in the early exploration of the area, the pursuit of plants. Johnson was a 'citizen and apothecarye of London' and one of the first men in England to take an interest in plants for purely botanical, rather than merely medicinal reasons. He toured Snowdonia in 1639 and later that year published *The Itinerary of a Botanist*, which included an account of his climb:

> . . . . we betook ourselves to our British Alps. The highest of all these is called Snowdon by the English, and Widhfa by the Britons. . . . . . . The whole mass of the mountain was veiled in cloud. . . . leaving our horses and outer garments, we began to climb the mountain. The ascent at first is difficult, but after a bit a broad open space is found, but equally sloping, great precipices on the left, and a difficult climb on the right. Having climbed three miles, we at last gained the highest ridge of the mountain, which was shrouded in thick cloud. Here the way was very narrow, and climbers are horror stricken by the rough rocky precipices on either hand and the Stygian marshes, both on this side and that. . . . . We sat down [on the summit] in the midst of the clouds, and first of all we arranged in order the plants we had, at our peril, collected among the rocks and precipices, and then we ate the food we had brought with us.

Johnson had two companions, a local guide and an interpreter. Another plant-hunting ascent of his—on Carnedd Llewelyn—was less successful because the guide refused to go to the cliffs 'where alone the rarer plants grew', saying he was afraid of eagles. Unfortunately

Johnson's first mountaineering trip to North Wales was also his last. He fought on the Royalist side in the Civil War and died of his wounds in 1644.

The plants of Snowdonia are particularly fascinating because, apparently, the variety of soil-conditions and weather which are gathered within an easily managed compass make it a sort of natural experimental laboratory. For more than three hundred years now botanists have found it a magnet. The twentieth-century hero of C. E. Montague's little masterpiece *In Hanging Garden Gully* pursued his quarry, a rare spiderwort, across a dangerous traverse, 'treading on air' on his single useful leg and getting his leader and the rope into a state of confused consternation. The flower that he sought was the most distinguished of Welsh plants, Lloydia serotina, named after its late-seventeenth-century discoverer, Edward Lloyd. He was keeper of the Ashmolean Museum in Oxford. He preferred the Welsh spelling of his name, Llwyd, often visited Snowdonia and explored the mountains more thoroughly than anyone before him. He made geographical as well as botanical discoveries. He it was, for example, who first described in print the rocky tumult at the top of Glyder Fach, and who first noted the infuriating mountaineering fact that there are many summits that seem to recede as one approaches them. He also exploded Camden's notion that Snowdonia is a land of perpetual snow.

The revival of scientific inquiry that distinguished the reign of Charles II brought an increasing number of visitors, among them the astronomer, Edmund Halley, who climbed Snowdon in 1697 to carry out some experiments. He did not enjoy the experience and described the area as 'this horrid spot of hills'.

The next century was more than half over before anyone went to Snowdonia for any other reasons than the antiquarian or the scientific. The honour of being the first man to go there for the modern motives, pleasure and exercise, goes to Lord George Lyttelton of Hagley in Worcestershire. He was a prominent politician, had been Chancellor of the Exchequer for a short time, and was able enough as a writer to earn a brief chapter in Dr Johnson's *Lives of the Poets* and to have Henry Fielding's novel *The History of Tom Jones* dedicated to him. In 1756 he made a strenous tour of North Wales, attended by his valet, 'so that I may, by this ramble, preserve a stock of health that may last all winter, and carry me through my parliamentary campaign.' His letters reveal an eye for beauty of various kinds.

> What Bala is most famous for is the beauty of its women and indeed I there saw some of the prettiest girls I ever beheld. The lake produces some very fine trout and a fish called whiting, peculiar to itself, and of so delicate a taste that I believe you would prefer the flavour of it to the lips of the fair maids of Bala.

He went into rhapsodies about the Vale of Ffestiniog—

> With the woman one loves, with the friend of one's heart, and a good study of books, one might pass an age here and think it a day.

—and he made one ascent, of Moel Hebog from Brynkir:

> On one side was midnight, on the other bright day;
> the whole extent of the mountain of Snowdon, on our
> left hand, was wrapped in clouds, from top to bottom;
> but on the right the sun shone most gloriously over
> the sea coast of Caernarvon. The hill we stood upon
> was perfectly clear, the way we came up a pretty easy
> ascent; but before us was a precipice of many hundred
> yards, and below, a vale, which, though not cultivated,
> had much savage beauty.

This is the voice of a new kind of traveller, observant and cheerful, keen to enjoy the changing moods of weather and landscape, free from his predecessors' concerns with what might be gleaned in the way of knowledge or wealth. Lyttelton was decades ahead of his time. His letters were written nearly twenty years before the publication of Thomas Gray's influential *Journal* of a tour in the Lake District, and he made his Snowdonian ramble nearly forty years before Captain Joseph Budworth, a man with an equally acute appreciation of pretty girls and good food as well as the pleasures of mountain scrambling, tackled the Lakeland fells in the same spirit.

The closing decades of the eighteenth century saw a revolution in the way men looked at mountains. No longer were they simply places of refuge as a desperate resort, regions of mystery and terror to be visited only by shepherds or, most infrequently, by men in search of special knowledge. Jean-Jacques Rousseau had proclaimed the romantic revolution, the superior virtue of all things natural and simple and wild. The classical shibboleths of 'man-made order and regularity were relaxing their grip on the imagination. Quite suddenly, men's eyes were opened to the elevating beauty of savage scenery.

The movement was strong enough to affect the attitude even of so sturdy a protagonist of the old values as Dr Samuel Johnson himself. He became, in his later years, a traveller of dedication and fortitude. He made his famous journey to the Western Islands of Scotland, at the instigation of Boswell, in the autumn of 1773. The following year, with his wealthy friends the Thrales, Dr Johnson went to North Wales, by way of Derbyshire, Chester, Denbigh, Bangor and Caernarvon. He ventured into the mountain area only once, to visit Dolbadarn Castle. In September Boswell wrote him a letter, trying, as ever, to provoke some majestic utterance:

> Wales has probably detained you longer than I supposed. You will have become quite a mountaineer, by visiting Scotland one year and Wales another. You must next go to Switzerland. Cambria will complain if you do not honour her also with some remarks.

But Johnson's response was disappointing. Perhaps he was not amused at being called a 'mountaineer' for in his own dictionary he had given the word the secondary definition: 'A savage; a free booter; a rustick.' Or perhaps he felt he had made his definitive pronouncement on mountaineering on the occasion of his visit to Ilam in Derbyshire a few months earlier:

> The ideas which it forces upon the mind are, the sublime, the dreadful and the vast. Above is inaccessible altitude, below is horrible profundity. Its grandeur is tempered with softness; the walker congratulates his own arrival at the place, and is grieved to think he must ever leave it. As he looks up to the rocks, his thoughts are el-

evated; as he turns his eyes on the vallies, he is composed and soothed. He that mounts the precipices wonders how he came thither, and doubts how he shall return. His walk is an adventure, and his departure an escape. He has not the tranquillity, but the horrors of solitude; a kind of turbulent pleasure, between fright and admiration.

Eight years after Dr Johnson's visit a Welsh antiquarian and naturalist, Thomas Pennant, published his guide-book, *'Journey to Snowdon'*. Dr Johnson said Pennant was 'the best traveller I ever read'. Certainly his book about Snowdonia —and he was the first writer to apply the word to the whole mountain range—was much the most reliable of the time, full and detailed, pleasantly written and accurate, based on first-hand knowledge. In the flood of tourist-journalism that now began to pour from the printing presses to meet the demands of the new travellers, it shines like a good deed in a naughty world, though Pennant himself was not above an occasional attack of the fashionable 'gothick' horrors. Cwm Idwal, for example, he describes as 'a fit place to inspire murderous thoughts, environed with horrible precipices'.

The imaginative excesses of most of the travel writers of that time have been a continuous source of amazement and amusement to later readers. It is, perhaps, unfair—hubristic even—to laugh too contemptuously at the quirks of a former fashion. But many of them were temptingly silly. Thomas Gray had no notion of what he was starting when he went to the Scottish Highlands in 1765 and wrote of the mountains: 'None but those monstrous creatures of God know how to join so much beauty with so much horror.' But he had tapped a rich vein of fantasy. Joseph Craddock, for example, in the 1770s, saw the Pass of Aberglaslyn as 'the last Approach to the mansion of Pluto through the regions of Despair'. And in 1795 Mr T. Hucks clambered up the innocuous Penmaenmawr mountain and recorded:

We rashly took the resolution to venture up this stupendous mountain without a guide, and therefore unknowingly fixed upon the most difficult part to ascend, and consequently were continually impeded by a vast number of unexpected obstructions. At length we surmounted every danger and difficulty, and safely arrived at the top. .

. . . In the midst of my melancholy cogitations I fully expected that the genius of the mountain would have appeared to me in some formidable shape and have reproached me with rashly presuming to disturb the sacred silence of his solitary reign.

There were many tourists coming to Snowdonia by this time, and not all of them in such a fevered state of mind. The young William Wordsworth, with his college friend from Cambridge, Robert Jones, made a three-week pedestrian tour in the summer of 1791 and climbed Snowdon from Beddgelert by moonlight to watch the dawn from the summit—a popular excursion of the period. A few years later Samuel Taylor Coleridge, soon to become Wordsworth's great friend and in-spirer, walked the area. And in 1798 an important milestone was reached—the first recorded rock climb in Britain.

It took place, impressively, on the most formidable rock face in Snowdonia—Clogwyn du'r Arddu, 'the black cliff of the black height', that lies a mile north-west of the summit of Snowdon. Once again, the motive was botany.

The Rev. William Bingley had made a number of mountain expedi-tions in Snowdonia with his friend, the Rev. Peter Williams, Rector of Llanrug and Llanberis, in search of plant specimens and botanical knowledge. Williams seems to have been the more daring of the two—he alarmed his companion on one occasion on Tryfan by jumping across from Adam, one of the two summit boulders above the cliff, to the other one, Eve. Bingley's description of their ascent of what must have been the East Terrace of Clogwyn du'r Arddu has become one of the most quoted passages in British mountaineering history:

I wandered to Clogwyn du'r Arddu (*Plate 1*), to search that rock for some plants which Lewyd and Ray have described as growing there. The Reverend Mr. Williams accompanied me, and he started the wild idea of attempting to climb up the precipice. I was too eager in my pursuit to object to the adventure, and we began our laborious task without once reflecting on the dangers that might attend it. For a little while we got on without much difficulty, but we were soon obliged to have recourse both to our hands and knees, in clamber-ing from one crag to another. Every step now required the utmost

1. *The Eastern Terrace (the diagonally sloping ledge in the centre of the picture) of Clogwyn du'r Arddu. (Photograph by Carl Rogers.)*

caution, and it was necessary to try that every stone was firm in its place before the weight of the body was trusted upon it. I had once lain hold of a piece of the rock, and was in the act of raising myself upon it, when it loosened from its bed, and I should have been precipitated headlong, had I not in a moment snatched hold of a tuft of rushes, and saved myself. When we had ascended somewhat more than halfway, there seemed no chance of our being able to proceed much farther, on account of the increasing size of the masses of rock above us. We rested a moment from our labour to consider what was to be done. The danger of again descending was much too great, for us to think of attempting it, unless we found it absolutely impossible to proceed. On looking down, the precipice, for at least three hundred feet, seemed almost perpendicular. We were eager in our botanical pursuit, and extremely desirous to be at the top, but I believe it was the prospect downwards that determined us to brave every difficulty. It happened fortunately that the steep immediately above us was the only one that presented any material danger. Mr. Williams having on a pair of strong shoes with nails in them, which would hold their footing better than mine, requested to make the first attempt, and after some difficulty he succeeded. We had along with us a small basket to contain our provisions, and hold the roots of such plants as we wished to transfer to his garden; this he carried behind him by means of a leathern belt fastened round his waist. When, therefore, he had fixed himself securely to a part of the rock, he took off his belt, and holding firmly by one end, gave the other to me: I laid hold, and, with a little aid from the stones, fairly pulled myself up by it. After this we got on pretty well, and in about an hour and a quarter from the commencement of our labour, found ourselves on the brow of this dreadful precipice, and in possession of all the plants we expected to find.

It was an impressive exploit with many elements that were to become familiar to rock climbers a century later—the use of hands and knees, the unreliable rock, the decision to go on because they dared not go back, the nailed shoes and even the judicious use of an artificial aid, the leather belt. But it had no real influence on the history of the sport. The two clergymen had climbed but not for climbers' reasons. They did not venture again on rock so steep and exposed. They inspired no followers. It was to be a long time before anyone clambered up steep rock in Snowdonia again; and even longer before another ascent was made on Clogwyn du'r Arddu.

Chapter III

THE MOUNTAINEERS ARRIVE

Fire made them, earth clothed them,
man found them, our playmates, the princes of hills.

FOUR years after the two clergymen made, inadvertently, the first recorded rock climb in Britain, a young poet made the first recorded rock climb in England. On August 4th, 1802, Samuel Taylor Coleridge took the shortest way from the summit of Scafell to Mickledore. He describes lowering himself as far as possible from successive ledges and dropping the rest of the way, 'my whole Limbs, in a *Tremble'*. His route was recognizably what is now called Broad Stand. And the spirit in which he scrambled about the fells—alone, travelling light, undeterred by bad weather or difficult terrain—is recognizably that of modern mountaineering. He walked the hills for the same motive that was to inspire the Snowdonia climbers a hundred years later—escape from ordinary, routine, health-giving exercise, and the exploration and stimulation of his innermost spirit:

> The farther I ascend from animated Nature, from men, and cattle, and the common birds of the woods and fields, the greater becomes in me the Intensity of the feeling of Life.

Unfortunately, Coleridge did not stay long in the Lake District. Poor health, a growing addiction to opium and a failing marriage drove him away. So his climb on Scafell, like that of Bingley and Williams on Clogwyn du'r Arddu, was nothing more than a singular achievement.

There is a pleasant significance, however, in the fact that the first two recorded rock climbs in this country should have been shared between Snowdonia and the Lake District. These are still the chief rock climbing areas in Britain south of the Scottish Highlands. It was on their cliffs, with gathering speed as the nineteenth century drew to its close, that the sport emerged and developed. Something like a rivalry, usually friendly but not always so, grew up between them.

The initial advantage lay with the Lake District. It was closer to centres of population, Kendal and Barrow, Penrith and Carlisle. It was more easily reached, by road and then by rail, from the big cities to the south. And in Pillar Rock in Ennerdale it had one summit that could not be attained without some exposed and strenuous scrambling.

Snowdonia had no comparable attraction to offer and it was, for many years, much harder to reach. Such roads as there were in the eighteenth century were described as 'public ditches or stepladders'. H. P. Wyndham, who toured the region in the 1770s and praised its 'romantic beauties', went on to say:

> Notwithstanding this, the Welsh tour has been hitherto strangely neglected; for while the English roads are crowded with travelling parties of pleasure, the Welsh are so rarely visited that the author did not meet with a single party during his six weeks journey through Wales. We must account for this from the general prejudice which prevails, that the Welsh roads are impracticable, the inns intolerable, and the people insolent and brutish.

Slowly the prejudices were overcome and the causes of them removed. The roads to the towns, Llanberis, Capel Curig and Beddgelert, were improved to encourage the carriage trade. The number of visitors increased steadily, so much so that by the summer of 1798 the Rev. W. Bingley could report:

> There is an inn at almost every respectable town, where postchaises are kept; but owing to the great numbers who now make this fashionable tour, delays are at times unavoidably occasioned by their all being employed.

After the turn of the century roads began to be made through the great passes. The carriage road from Capel Curig to Bangor was opened in 1805, and the Nant Ffrancon Pass became part of the important mail coach route to Holyhead and Ireland. In 1826 Telford's suspension bridges across the River Conway and the Menai Straits were completed. Four years later the final link was forged in the road network we know today with the building of a carriage road over the Llanberis Pass.

Before these developments most of Snowdon's visitors had set off from points south of the mountain, Beddgelert and Snowdon Ranger. Now Llanberis took over as the principal tourist centre and was given a boost in 1832 when the ambitious Duchess of Kent, making a premature royal progress, presented her thirteen year-old daughter, Princess Victoria, to the people of the village. The pony track—along the route which the mountain railway now follows—offered the least laborious approach to the highest summit in England and Wales. The middle years of the century brought still more tourists, and with them, inevitably, the start of the continuing despoliation of Y Wyddfa. When the first tourists reached the summit of Snowdon they found a small, level, stony area, surrounded by a low wall, with a small cairn marking the high point. About 1820 part of the wall was demolished and the stones used to build 'a wretched vile hut' a few yards below the cairn, to provide shelter and, later, simple refreshment. Soon after that the Ordnance Survey constructed the massive summit cairn which stands to this day.

When George Borrow, the great linguist and traveller, ascended Snowdon by the Llanberis path in 1854 he found:

The Wyddfa is about thirty feet in diameter and is surrounded on three sides by a low wall. In the middle of it is a rude cabin, in which refreshments are sold, and in which a person resides throughout the year, though there are few or no visitors to the hill's top, except during the months of summer.

His daughter, Henrietta, had 'some excellent coffee' in the cabin. Borrow and his guide, a young lad he had hired in Llanberis, shared 'a bottle of tolerable ale'.

Although the main paths up Snowdon were clearly marked by this time and there was no shortage of guide-books and maps, it was still customary for visitors to employ the services of a local guide for their more serious ventures. The guides were called 'rangers'. They might be local shepherds or hotel servants. Their fees were modest, their duties often involved little more than chivvying the ponies along, and—like their Alpine counterparts—they did not always give satisfaction. But some of them earned a high reputation. There was 'honest William Roberts', for example, of the Dolbadarn Hotel, who was said to have made two thousand ascents of Snowdon in twenty years of guiding, with 'a brigandish hat on his head, a knapsack or large wallet on his shoulders (well strapped over the chest), and a stout stick in his hand'. And on the western side of the mountain, there was John Morton who opened the Snowdon Ranger Inn beside Llyn Cwellyn to accommodate his clients.

When George Borrow encountered Morton, who called himself as well as his inn 'the Snowdon Ranger', he provoked a strong response by asking if many people ascended Snowdon from his house:

> 'Not so many as I could wish,' said the ranger; 'people in general prefer ascending Snowdon from that trumpery place Beth Gelert; but those who do are fools—begging your honour's pardon. The place to ascend Snowdon from is my house. The way from my house up Snowdon is wonderful for the romantic scenery which it affords; that from Beth Gelert can't be named in the same day with it for scenery; moreover, from my house you may have the best guide in Wales; whereas the guides of Beth Gelert—but I say nothing. If your honour is bound for the Wyddfa, as I suppose you are, you had better start from my house tomorrow under my guidance.'

Another guide of repute was Henry Owen *(Plate 3)*, whom everyone called Harry, and he was another who operated from his own hostelry, the Pen-y-Gwryd Hotel *(Plate 2)*. The Pen-y-Gwryd started life soon after the road was built over Llanberis Pass as a

> . . . . small public house, with a sign signifying nothing, a small parlour with half a dozen hair-bottomed chairs and a mahogany table,

2. The Pen-y-Gwryd Hotel, birthplace of Snowdonia climbing. The step-ladders were to help people to climb into the wagonette. The doorway where the group are standing was sealed up in the 1930ís because the Capel Curig road had become too busy with traffic. (Photograph by the Abraham brothers.)

and a ladder-like staircase to a kind of cockloft, which was divided into two compartments, one for the family, the other fitted up for travellers.

It stood, as it stands today, 900 feet above sea level, at the junction of the Capel Curig—Beddgelert road with the eastern end of the Llanberis Pass. Its founder and first landlord was John Roberts of Pen y Bryn, Llanberis. But it was not until the long reign of Harry Owen, who took over from Roberts in 1847, that the Pen-y-Gwryd established itself as the centre of Snowdonia's first rock climbing community. There is probably no place in the world that can claim a longer or more honourable connection with the sport. It was a matter of luck, of course, that Owen's tenure should have coincided with the first flowering of the mountaineering impulse. His hotel offered quick access to the two main scrambling and climbing grounds of the pioneers: the Glyders and Tryfan to the north; and to the west Snowdon and the cliffs of Lliwedd and Clogwyn y Garnedd, Crib Goch and Dinas Mot and Cyrn Las. But it was his warm and friendly hospitality that created the Pen-y-Gwryd legend, in much the same way as Dan Tyson was to make a natural home for the first Lake District climbers at the Wastwater Hotel. In each case, the recipe was the same—a simple, comfortable inn, within easy reach of the big cliffs, under capable, steady and tolerant management.

Harry Owen was born on a farm in Nant Gwynant in 1822. When he was twenty-five he took the two decisive steps of his life; he bought Pen-y-Gwryd and he married a local girl called Ann Pritchard. Together they ran the hotel for the next forty years and more.

Little is known of their first years there. The vital pages of the visitors' book were torn out by vandals long ago. But it is on record that the Owens were hosts, in their first year, to two of the most influential men in the development of mountain exploration in Britain. One was, F. H. Bowring, a compulsive hill walker in the days when it was generally regarded as an eccentric aberration, who maintained his enthusiasm long enough to introduce Walter Parry Haskett Smith to Lakeland scrambling in the early 1880s and to be remembered by Geoffrey Young as

> ... a dignified and rather awesome figure, ascetic, remote, and straggle-bearded like a prophet. In the black morning coat, full grey trousers and low black stove-hat of our Victorian elders, he strode upon the hills he had wandered for fifty years.

The other visitor in 1847 was C. A. O. Baumgartner, a natural adventurer, one of the pioneer 'Pillarites' of the Lake District, and the first man known to have traversed the airy crest of the Crib Goch ridge. The hotel was still tiny, with two bedrooms for visitors and one sitting-room, a little parlour facing on to the Beddgelert road.

The first surviving entry in the visitors' book states simply:

Mr. Herbert Spencer, during a week's stay at Pen-y-Gwryd, has been made very comfortable, and is able to commend the attention and obligingness of Mr. and Mrs. Owen. 18 July 1855.

It is not clear whether this was the eminent philosopher, but there is no doubt at all of the identities of the eminent men who stayed there the following year. They were the cleric and novelist Charles Kingsley who had just published *Westward Ho!*, Thomas Hughes who was soon to publish *Tom Brown's Schooldays*, and a playwright, Tom Taylor, who was later to become editor of *Punch*.

Kingsley had been there before. In his book *Mountains with a Difference*, Geoffrey Young tells how his father 'had found Pen-y-Gwryd in its primordial days' and discovered the pleasure of running down scree shoots with Kingsley. Now Kingsley organized his 1856 visit to what he called 'the divinest pig-sty beneath the canopy'.

The three friends reached the hotel, in the highest of spirits, on August 12th. They were more interested in the fishing than the mountaineering but despite this, and despite the unrelenting severity of the weather, they clambered about on Snowdon and Glyder Fawr and enjoyed themselves in the unselfconscious way which seemed to come easily to the more prosperous Victorians. They composed a series of rough, rumbustious verses for the visitors' book in praise of the region and Pen-y-Gwryd. Kingsley gave a vivid picture of the hotel in his novel *Two Years Ago* which was published the following year:

. . . soon he saw slate roofs glittering in the moonlight, and found himself at the little inn of Pen-y-Gwryd, at the meeting of the three great valleys, the central heart of the mountains. And a genial, jovial little heart it is, and an honest, kindly little heart too, with warm life-blood within. . . . He strode hastily in, and down the little passage to the kitchen. It was a low room, ceiled with dark beams, from which hung bacon and fishing-rods, harness and drying stockings, and all the miscellanea of a fishing inn kept by a farmer, and beneath it the usual, happy, hearty, honest group. There was Harry Owen, bland and stalwart, his baby in his arms, smiling upon the world in general; old Mrs Pritchard bending over the fire, putting the last touch to one of those miraculous soufflets, compact of clouds and nectar, which transport alike palate and fancy, at the first mouthful, from Snowdon to Belgrave Square.

Mrs Pritchard was, of course, Mrs Owen's mother who helped out during the season. Mrs Owen herself, described as 'handsome and ladylike', comes bustling in from the kitchen a moment later. 'Three tuneful Snowdon guides' have just concluded a three-part rendering of 'The Rising of the Lark'. Harry Owen has been up Snowdon that day and is due to set off again at midnight with a German client who wants to see the sunrise.

The hotel visitors' book charts the rising popularity of the place, especially among public school and university men. Holiday reading parties were fashionable in those days and two undergraduates from New College, Oxford, record that the hotel 'is much too nice a place to read at'. A group of masters from Winchester College became regular visitors, and against the name of one of them a later hand wrote, 'Many a licking I've had from you.' Many of the entries were, in the nature of these things, hopelessly trivial or weakly facetious, but one of them at least—dated July 20th 1874—stands out as a lapidary example of the genre at its best:

> Been up Snowdon,
> A nice ascent;
> William Boden,
> Burton-on-Trent.

Fishing was the main attraction in the early days and it was this that brought John Henry Cliffe to Snowdonia in 1840. For the next twenty years or so he returned regularly. In his book *Notes and Recollections of an Angler* he described a man whose expeditions were more adventurous than his own:

> Picture to yourself a tall man about 52 years of age, of a wiry, spare habit, rather slightly built, dressed in a pair of dingy slop trousers, a linen spencer of the same complexion, without hat or covering of any sort for the head, no necktie, his shirt-collar unbuttoned, with an enormous *Alpenstock* or climbing pole, seven or eight feet in length,

3. *Harry Owen and his wife Ann at the Pen-y-Gwryd Hotel.*
(Photographer unknown.)

in his hand, and you may perhaps be able to form some idea of the strange grotesque figure we have endeavoured to describe. His object was, to use his own expression, 'to follow the skyline' of every mountain he visited. For example, he would ascend Snowdon from Llanberis, but instead of following the beaten track, he would take the edge of the mountain along the verge of the highest precipices, following what he called the 'skyline' until he reached the summit; he would then descend the other side of the mountain towards Beddgelert, in a similar manner. He most frequently performed his excursions alone, although occasionally, when not so familiar with the locality, he availed himself of the services of a guide. He would follow up these rambles *de die in diem*, regardless of the weather, and was generally on his legs from about 9a.m. until 8p.m. The most extraordinary thing was, how he could keep up such violent daily exercise without any refreshment whatever during the period he was among the mountains. To prevent thirst, he carried a small pebble in his mouth; and Henry Owen, the guide, assured us that he never saw him partake of anything to eat or drink, not even a cup of cold water, whilst on an excursion. We have several times met him on his return to the inn, drenched with perspiration, and whilst his dinner was being prepared, he would continue a gentle exercise (staff in hand), to 'cool down'—like a racehorse after a 'breather'—preparatory to taking of his repast—in fine weather generally *alfresco*—exhibiting not the least apparent fatigue. He was a man of very temperate habits: two or three glasses of sherry were the extent of his libations; he avoided smoking, and he would be up early in the morning performing his ablutions for several hours. He appeared to have no other object in climbing to the wild mountain tops than merely (as he said) to behold the wonderful works of the Almighty. Such was the remarkable individual with whom we became acquainted at Pen-y-Gwryd. We found him a most refined, intellectual companion, well-read and informed on all subjects of general interest, thoroughly versed in Welsh topography, and in his demeanour most affable and courteous. He informed us that he spent several weeks annually in North Wales, following up the same pursuit—mountain-climbing, either revisiting old scenes or finding out, if possible, some fresh mountain path still more difficult and arduous to surmount, than what he had previously attempted. In following the 'skyline' no rocks, however rough, no precipices—unless perfectly inaccessible—ever daunted him. This singular mania or hobby-horse, he appears to have followed up for years, and continued with unabated ardour. The last time we saw him was on a wet, stormy morning, preparing to 'hie away to the mountain's brow', on his route from Pen-y-Gwryd to Capel Curig; the said route

4. *The Clogwyn y Person Atête and the easy but airy ridge of the Parson's Nose.* *(Photograph by Carl Rogers.)*

being the 'skyline' over the summit and entire length of the lofty Moel Siabod.

This was the famous but mysterious 'Climbing Parson'—Snowdonia's clerical counterpart of the Lake District's 'Patriarch of the Pillarites', the Rev. James Jackson. But he lacked Jackson's genius for self-advertisement, and no one has ever discovered who he was. Even F. H. Bowring, who knew more about the hills of Britain than anyone else at the time, never came across him though he often heard tell of him. Tradition, however, has generously credited the elusive 'Climbing Parson' with the first ascent of the northern spur of Crib y Ddysgl, which is called the Parson's Nose (*Plate 4*). If he did do it—and it would nicely accord with his predilection for skylines—it was a surprisingly bold enterprise for the time. And it would explain, as nothing else has done, the origin of the clift's name, Clogwyn y Person, the Parson's Cliff.

The key year in this period was 1854. For the British people, it was the year when they plunged—with a militaristic enthusiasm that was soon to be shattered—into the Crimean War. In the history of mountaineering, it was the year when a young English barrister called Alfred Wills climbed the Wetterhorn in the Bernese Oberland—an ascent which has been generally taken to mark the opening of the 'Alpine Golden Age'. And it was the year when another young lawyer paid his first visit to Pen-y-Gwryd.

His name was C. E. Mathews. His visit to the hotel in the spring of 1854 was the first of many. He was to climb Snowdon and Cader Idris more than a hundred times each. His mountaineering career was to span half a century and more and prove—powerfully influential, not so much for his climbing which was more creative in the Alps than in North Wales, but by virtue of his great 'clubbability'.

It was around Mathews that the first Snowdonia mountaineers formed their, first club, which he named 'The Society of Welsh Rabbits'. Nearly thirty years later he was to be a prime mover in the formation of the Climbers' Club and become its first President. Geoffrey Young described him in these words:

> A romantic lover of hills and climbing, he showed praiseworthy energy in encouraging others to share his lifelong enthusiasm, and a Victorian absolutism as to the fashion in which they should do so. A man of liberal mind and one of Joe Chamberlain's closest friends and political supporters, he was one of the very few great Alpine pioneers who cared almost equally for home climbing and who put his authority behind its development.

Charles Edward Mathews was one of those Protean Victorians whose lives, for their sheer variety and confidence and vitality, can only arouse wonder and envy in this more tentative age. He had, in a sense, every advantage—born in an age when Britain led the Western world and ruled much of the rest, in one of the leading cities in commercial and industrial progress, into a social class that flourished as never before and believed it was showing the way to Utopia. Born in Birmingham and trained in the law, he became a partner in a firm of successful solicitors. He played an active role in many spheres. Ronald Clark, in his book *The Victorian Mountaineers*, wrote:

> Mathews was a founder of the National Education League. He was chairman of innumerable committees, president of innumerable societies, a leader in local politics, a justice of the Peace, and an active and opinionated member of a whole galaxy of bodies. He managed to pack all this activity into seventy-one crowded years, to become also, as well as one of the most accomplished mountaineers of his day, an expert of importance on subjects as varied as the Waterloo Campaign, the Birmingham Water Supply, and the detailed history of Mont Blanc.

Mountaineering was a family tradition. It was at his uncle William's house on the outskirts of Birmingham that the Alpine Club was born in the autumn of 1857. A high proportion of those present were members of the Mathews family, and the young Charles Edward was one of them. He had already enjoyed two Alpine seasons and begun a partnership with the guide, Melchior Anderegg of Meyringen, which was to last more than twenty years. Throughout his career he remained an Alpinist rather than a rock climber. His visits to Pen-y-Gwryd took place, almost invariably, at Christmas or Easter, when conditions of snow and ice might be expected. He was a convivial man, fond of company in the mountains and around the fire in the evenings, addicted to dinners and reunions. As a founder member of the Alpine Club and later the Club President, it was he more than anyone else who introduced the Alpine fraternity to winter mountaineering in Snowdonia during the 1860s and 1870s.

There were Alpinists, of course, who considered the British mountains beneath their dignity, but the list of those who went from time to time to Pen-y-Gwryd is a distinguished one. The Pendlebury brothers came there, and Charles Pilkington, the pioneer of guidleless climbing in the Alps, and Frederick Morshead whom Geoffrey Young described as 'perhaps the finest and fastest Alpinist of his day'. Clinton Dent the writer and H. G. Willink the artist were also of the company. It included two of the men, Horace Walker and A. W. Moore, who accompanied Mathews on the first ascent of the Brenva Ridge in 1865. And at the very beginning of the period, in December 1860, the impressive trio of Professor Tyndall, Professor Huxley and Mr Busk turned up at the hotel.

Tyndall and Huxley were eminent scientists who had first visited the Alps for reasons of research but had quickly come to love mountaineering for its own sake. Snowdonia was deep in snow so they bought rake handles, for fourpence each, at Bethesda and got a blacksmith to fashion them into serviceable alpenstocks. They engaged Robert Hughes as their guide and attacked Snowdon by the ordinary route from Pen-y-Pass, forcing their way through a cornice on to the summit ridge. They gained the summit at three in the afternoon, and Tyndall later described their feelings in an article for the *Saturday Review*:

> Above and behind us the heavens were of the densest grey; towards the western horizon this was broken by belts of fiery red, which, nearer to the sun, brightened to orange and yellow. The mountains of Flintshire were flooded with glory, and later on, through the gaps in the ranges, the sunlight was poured in coloured beams, which could be tracked through the air to the places on which their radiance fell. The scene would bear comparison with the splendour of the Alps themselves.

Tyndall's enthusiasm was influential but it was the sustained interest of C. E. Mathews that made Pen-y-Gwryd's name. From 1861 onwards he went there almost every year. He was still going, though more occasionally, forty years later when he set down his 'Reminiscences of Pen-y-Gwryd' for the editor of *The Climbers' Club Journal*:

> How well I remember Harry Owen doing Punch for his children in the same old kitchen, Mrs. Owen knitting in the corner, and the collie dogs lying on the floor. No hot whisky was ever so delicious as that which we drank over the peat fire, while the wind was howling or the rain was beating outside. No talk was ever more manly, no friendships were ever more sincere.

If I were to set down the number of times I have been on the top of Snowdon, my readers would probably suspect me of exaggeration, so I forbear. But in company with the late Mr. Adams-Reilly, one of the most gifted of men, and with my life-long friend, Mr. Frederick Morshead of Winchester, one of the ablest mountaineers of his time, I certainly was the pioneer of regular winter climbing, at Pen-y-Gwryd. Our names appear January 14 to 17, 1870. At that time of the year we were quite certain of having the inn to ourselves; we almost always found snow on the hills; the rivers were usually in flood. It was an enchanting experience, and yet, will it be believed? Some Solon on tour at a later period of the year was good enough to append the following note to our names: —'What an ass a fellow must be to come to such a place in January.' It was at this date that we founded the 'Society of Welsh Rabbits,' the object of which was to explore Snowdonia in winter, and for many years, as near Christmas time as possible, the Rabbits met at Pen-y-Gwryd. Mr. Adams-Reilly designed a coat of arms for the Society. He was an accomplished artist, and his design, beautifully executed in pen and ink, was for some time on the wall of the dining-room, but, of course, was ultimately stolen.

The Rabbits met frequently and, true to their name, multiplied rapidly. In 1879 Mathews gathered twenty-five members of the Alpine Club for a winter meet in Snowdonia. In the next decade they introduced some of their Alpine guides to Welsh climbing (*Plate 5*). Gabriel Taugwalder of Zermatt was there and Aloys Supersaxs of Saas. And in his 'Reminiscences', Mathews recalled the occasion when his own Alpine mentor confronted Snowdon:

On the 2nd of April, 1888, I was again at Pen-y-Gwryd with Dent, Walker, Morshead and Mortimer. These gentlemen had been staying with me at a lovely cottage I then occupied in the valley of the Llyffnant, near Machynlleth. I had with me, as a guest, the greatest of Swiss guides, Melchior Anderegg of Meyringen, and he accompanied us on an ascent of Snowdon by way of Crib Goch. I led all the way, and as the snow was deep and very soft, it was not an altogether easy task. In one place I hesitated for a few seconds. Melchior

5. *C. E. Mathews, pioneer of the Snowdonia climbing community, and his Alpine guide for more than 20 years, Melchior Anderegg. The picture was taken in 1880. (Photographer unknown.)*

6. *The Crib Goch ridge leading to the summit of Crib y Ddysgl and then (left, background) to Y Wyddfa, the summit of Snowdon. (Photograph by Carl Rogers.)*

instantly forged to the front and proffered his services, which I emphatically declined. 'No,' I said, 'I am guide to-day, and you are the Herr.' On reaching the summit of Crib Goch, there was the peak of Snowdon on our left, a great white cone rising into a blue sky. Melchior, whose knowledge of Swiss distances is faultless, at once said: 'We must go back; we cannot climb the final peak in less than five or six hours.' 'Oh, yes,' I said, 'we shall be there in an hour.' 'That, sir,' was his reply 'is quite impossible.' In five minutes over the hour we were on the top of Snowdon *(Plate 6).*

The incursion of the Alpinists, and especially the fact that they went there out of the normal tourist season, established the fortunes of the hotel, and made it both possible and necessary to improve its facilities. In 1859 a coffee room was added, and the old building was given a new roof. Sometime in the 1880s a complete new wing was built, the south-facing wing where the hotel entrance now stands. By 1890 the Owens were prosperous enough to have hot water piped into every bedroom—a very advanced feature for the time—and install the magnificent bath, complete with metal canopy and controls for shower and all-round spray, which is still in grateful use.

Efforts were made to rescue the visitors' book from the depredations of the vulgar. Such pages as had survived were carefully, collated and repaired and specially bound into seven stout volumes. In 1884 Mr Hugo J. Young presented the Owens with a thick, black, quarto book, with a metal lock, for serious 'contributions on mountain rambles, botany, geology and other subjects of interest connected with Pen-y-Gwryd, with reminiscences, poetical and otherwise'. This is the famous Locked Book. There can be no mistaking its purpose. At the top right-hand corner of the front cover, the words are inscribed 'Not the Visitors' Book'. And on the first page stands Hugo Young's dedication:

April 10th, 1884.

Dear Mr. and Mrs. Owen,

On my visits to Pen-y-Gwryd I have noticed that your visitors' book has become the receptacle for all sorts of nonsense scribbled by the casual passer-by.

On the other hand, many notes are recorded of lasting use and interest to many who delight to stay weeks with you.

It would, I think, be an advantage to keep the two distinct, and I now have the pleasure to present you with a separate book, not to be used at all as a record of visitors' names, but which I hope you may live to see filled with contributions which it will be a pleasure to read. I have provided it with a lock, that by exercising control over the key you may preserve its pages from abuse.

Please accept it in remembrance of the pleasant days I have spent with you, and your never-failing attention.

Yours truly,
H. J. Y.

The book has admirably served Young's purpose. It contains fascinating entries in the handwriting of many of the leading spirits of rock climbing: Stocker and Wall, Archer Thomson and Eckenstein, O. G. Jones and George Abraham and Geoffrey Young, then Tony Moulam in the 1950s and the Everest men of 1953 testing their oxygen apparatus and finding it 'a dismal business', the young Chris Bonington recording some of his early new routes, and details of Eric Beard's record-breaking run round the Snowdon Horseshoe in one hour forty minutes on October 7th, 1961. For anyone interested in the way rock climbing developed in Snowdonia, the Locked Book is a unique and invaluable primary source.

Harry Owen died in May 1891 after forty-four years as landlord. His wife Ann died five years later and was buried beside him in Beddgelert churchyard. After their time the hotel entered upon a confused and troubled period and the centre of climbing interest moved up the hill to Pen-y-Pass.

Mathews went to Pen-y-Gwryd in April, 1901, nearly half a century after his first visit:

> I found myself the only visitor at the Inn. I toiled up the mountain when deep snow was lying between Glas Llyn and the summit. On my return I missed, with profound sadness, the beaming faces and the warm welcome to which I had been accustomed for so many years. Where was Mrs. Pritchard, who made pan-cakes for me in my younger days? Where was the gallant Harry Owen and his buxom and charming wife? Where were Catherine and Jane, their daughters; the most willing waitresses who ever attended to the wants of man? Where were the friends who climbed with me in midwinter on Snowdon and Lliwedd, on Crib Goch and Siabod, on the Carnedds and the Glyders, in the days that are no more?
>
> It required but little effort of the imagination to conjure up the ghosts of the departed. I could almost see their 'old familiar faces.' I could almost feel the pressure of their hands. I could almost hear the honest happy laughter I remember so well. Alas! for Pen-y-Gwryd. One custodian only was in charge, and he was 'in possession on behalf of the receiver.'

Chapter IV

THE CONQUEST OF LLIWEDD

---

*. . . racing the wind and sun, rapturous-eyed,
to conquer Lliwedd by its leaning side.*

THROUGHOUT the 1860s and 70s and beyond, many Alpine mountaineers sought winter practice in Snowdonia and the Lake District. Of the two they seem to have preferred Snowdonia, where they could make longer and more rewarding expeditions.

Yet it was in the Lake District, on the crags around Wasdale Head, that British rock climbing emerged as a separate sport in its own right. And it was not the creation of the Alpine fraternity, but of a partnership between local dalesmen and holiday visitors from the cities of England, particularly in the early stages the partnership between John Wilson Robinson, a farmer from Lorton, and Walter Parry Haskett Smith who was to be called 'the father of British rock climbing'.

Hasket Smith first went to Wasdale head in the summer vacation of 1881 with a reading party of fellow students from Oxford. There he met the veteran and inveterate hill wanderer, F. H. Bowring, who showed him the delights of exploring the fells off the beaten tracks. He returned the next summer with his younger brother, Edmund, and together they clambered up some of the easier gullies on Great End and Pavey Ark and Pillar Rock and made an attempt on the big North wall of Pillar Rock. In 1884 he was back again and Bowring introduced him to Robinson. The next year Robinson and another local man, George

Seatree, made the first use of what they called 'the Alpine rope' on Lakeland rock. And in June 1886, Haskett Smith made his justly famous solo first ascent of Napes Needle on Great Gable. Within ten years of Haskett Smith's appearance in the Lakes, a small but growing and enthusiastic community of rock climbers had come together and made dozens of routes on the virtually virgin cliffs of Scafell and Gable and Pillar Rock. Some of the routes are still graded 'Severe' and one of them—Eagle's Nest Ridge Direct on Gable is still graded 'Very Severe (Mild)'.

Their achievement is the more impressive in view of the conditions in which they were climbing. Their equipment was nothing more than rough tweeds and nailed country boots and four-foot ice axes and sixty-foot lengths of hemp rope which they had little idea how to use to any advantage. The crags were more dangerous and often more difficult than they are today, snared with loose rocks and stones and slimy vegetation which have been cleared away now by the succeeding generations. Above all, of course, they were venturing where no men had ever been before. They had no maps or guide-books or, indeed, any assurance that a climbable way would be found. There was no body of accumulated experience to guide them as to the capabilities of the human body and nerve in high, steep places. It was exploration on several levels at once, and although they started in the safer-seeming gullies they were soon moving out on ribs and ridges and open walls, and though their equipment and techniques were so palpably rudimentary they worked, with ever-increasing daring, for more than twenty years without a single fatal climbing accident.

The advance in North Wales was much more tentative at first. Such activity as there was centred largely, though not exclusively, on Lliwedd, the big rambling cliff to the east of Snowdon's summit which towers up to 1,000 feet above Llyn Llydau and was to prove the chief preoccupation of the Snowdonia climbers until the outbreak of the First World War (*Plates 7 and 8*).

Lliwedd is one of those rare cliffs which are possibly rather less frequented today than they were seventy years ago. The reasons for its comparative unpopularity now are much the same as the reasons for its early popularity. It is a considerable way from the road. Though steep and challenging in places, it is of so broken and complicated a character that route-finding is as vital to success as climbing skill. Its appeal is to the explorer's instincts of the Alpinist rather than to the more specialized interests of the hard rock man. It was the first cliff in the world to have a climbing guide-book to itself—*The Climbs on Lliwedd* by J. M. Archer Thomson and A. W. Andrews which was published in 1909. In his introduction Andrews tried to describe and crystallize the mountain's attraction:

> Grand as the cliffs are in days of clear weather, or those rare moments of morning glory when 'the Hunter of the East has caught the crags of Lliwedd in a noose of light,' they are finer still when a half-drawn curtain of mist hides the mountain's secrets, revealing from time to time, as it lifts or sways with a passing breath of wind, some well-known landmark on the face.

> One of the principal charms of Lliwedd lies in the intricacy of its precipices. A climb on it is to nearly all a venture into the unknown, where 'mountaineering' is as essential as the power of ascending difficult rocks. Its problems are those of the great rock peaks of the Alps, and to attack them safely practice in descent is equally indispensable, for those who are unfamiliar with the mountain may well find that prudence sometimes counsels a retreat, either owing to unfavourable conditions or to failure to hit off the right method of tackling some difficult pitch. Obviously, less experienced climbers will attempt the easier climbs first, but an emphatic warning must be given to novices that steadiness is essential on all the routes of Lliwedd, easy and difficult alike, owing to the exposed character of the climbing.

> As a school for mountaineers Lliwedd is unrivalled.

The possibilities of Lliwedd were first noted by two men, T. H. Murray Browne and W. R. Browne, who made something of a speciality of pointing the way for others. In 1869 they had drawn attention, in the visitors' book at the Wastwater Hotel, to the challenge of Scafell Pinnacle. Three years later one of them made this entry in the Pen-y-Gwryd visitors' book:

7. *The size and complexity of Lliwedd made it the favourite cliff of the early Snowdonia climbers. It was first climbed in January 1883. By 1914 there were more than thirty distinct routes. (Photograph by Carl Rogers.)*

Tried to get up Lliwedd direct from Llyn Llydaw up the crags, but failed completely. Mounted eventually to the Col on the left. The direct ascent may be practicable, but I shall be glad to hear from anyone who achieves it. It has not, so far as I am aware, been done, and is certainly difficult.

Ten years elapsed before Lliwedd was next attempted, but this time a more determined assault was mounted. One of the protagonists, T. W. Wall, was a member of the Alpine Club and later published a full account in the Club's *Journal*:

In January, 1882, from the summit of Crib Goch, Mr. A. H. Stocker and myself were struck by the grand appearance of the Lliwedd cliffs, and hearing from Owen, the land-lord of the Pen-y-Gwryd Hotel, that the northern face had never been climbed, the desire to make the first ascent naturally came upon us.

They attempted it the next day, by way of the Central Gully—which was not climbed direct until 1938—and were driven back after 50 feet by rain and the exposed seriousness of the route. Clearly, though, they had something of the modern rock climber's possessive urge, for they gave Harry Owen an addressed postcard and made him promise to tip them off if anyone else showed an interest in the cliff. No one did and they were there again, one year later, 'with 80 feet of rope and our trusty axes'. This time they tried to force a route on the rocks to the west of the Central Gully. Wall wrote:

Three bits in particular may be mentioned as far the hardest, although they are more or less typical of these crags, which nowhere offer 20 consecutive yards of easy rock-work. The first difficulty which presented itself was where the ledge was broken by a bold face of rock. One of us was pushed to the top of the smooth part, and finding that he could not descend to the ledge on the other side, he ascended a little higher, anchored himself firmly to the rocks, assisted his companion up, and let him down to the required ledge; then, throwing the rope over a pinnacle, he gave both ends to his companion to hold tight, and slid down the 40 feet of rope to join him. After a few yards of easier work we came to a ledge about 6 inches wide and 4 yards long; the rock above was nearly perpendicular, with no handhold and there was nothing below. It was the only way; we could not turn it, and somehow we got over, but neither of us wishes to be there again. From that ever-to-be-remembered ledge the climbing was grand work up to the point where we had to turn from a westerly direction to go straight up the face. Here there was a nasty corner. A narrow ledge about 2 inches wide had below it a sloping face of rock with 3 minute cracks in it. One of us had crossed this in safety, and so assumed a position in which the rope would have been of very little use. He was then opposed by a steep bit, topped by 4 feet of perpendicular rock, with a very steep slope of heather above. At the moment that his last foot left the highest peg of rock his other knee slipped, and the heather, grass and earth began to give way in his left hand. It was an awkward moment, for the other

8. Lliwedd and some of its classic routes.

Features and routes on Lliwedd
EB   East Buttress
CG   Central Gully
WB   West Buttress
SG   Slanting Gully
1.   Horned Crag Route
2.   Avalanche (finishing on the Great Terrace)
3.   Mallory's Slab (finishing on the Bowling Green)
4.   Primitive Route

man was not well situated for supporting a jerk at the end of 30 feet of rope, which would mean a fall of about 50 feet. Happily the other knee got on the heather and the axe held firm in the earth. Our difficulties were then over.

There is a more laconic account in the Pen-y-Gwryd book:

Messrs. T. W. Wall and A. H. Stocker, after two attempts on Lliwedd by central gully, ascended North face by buttress West of central gully, hitting arête 13 yards from summit. No-one is recommended to attempt the ascent without at least 60 feet of rope. Height of rocks—about 850 feet: time taken—four hours and a half. Jan. 4, 1883.

No one has succeeded in discovering the precise route that Wall and Stocker followed. Archer Thompson who came to know the crag better than anyone else of the time believed they had used the Bilberry Terrace with a westerly variation. Whichever way they went, however, they had climbed Lliwedd for the first time. Clark and Pyatt, in their book *Mountaineering in Britain*, say it was 'the first major rock climb in Wales and one which was at least a decade in advance of its time. It was interesting, too, from a technical point of view, in the use of combined operations—'One of us was pushed to the top of the smooth part'—and in the use of rope techniques of a sophisticated good sense that the Lake District men were not to attain for many years.

But the climb started no fashion. In 1884 Stocker and another companion, A. G. Parker, made a second route—what is now called the Primitive Route and graded 'Just Difficult'. Stocker considered it easier than his first venture and described it, in the visitors' book, as:

...up central gully to the foot of the steep part, out by ledges on the right—then straight up the face, keeping gully to the left, arriving at the cairn . . . . All through the hand and foot hold is very good. The chief difficulties lie in the first 200 feet after leaving the gully.

After that, three years were to pass before the next recorded attempt on Lliwedd.

New men of mountaineering zeal were now arriving at Pen-y-Gwryd. E. R. Kidson of Birmingham signed the visitors' book on July

29th, 1883, marking the first of many visits. In the next twelve years he was to ascend Snowdon seventy times. Eighteen months later A. Evans of Manchester and W. E. Corlett of Liverpool made their first appearance and wrote in the book:

> The ascent from Glaslyn in winter up the zig-zag path to the summit ridge of Snowdon is positively dangerous and should not be attempted without spiked shoes and ice axes, with both of which we were unprovided.

In fact, Corlett slid about 150 feet down the slopes of Crib y Ddysgl towards the lake. But he returned with Evans the following year and they 'spent three-quarters of an hour scrambling up and down the Crib Goch pinnacles—they afford good crag-work but the rocks are very sharp and cut the fingers in an unpleasant manner.' The spring of 1887 introduced to the scene one of the most remarkable men in the story of British mountaineering—Oscar Johannes Ludwig Eckenstein, heavy alike in build and beard and manner, endlessly ingenious and inventive in practical matters, prickly and contentious and totally individualistic.

His father, a man of Socialist sympathies, had fled from the Rhineland to England in 1848. Oscar Eckenstein was born in Canonbury, London, in 1859 and educated at University College School in Gower Street. He studied chemistry at London University and then in Bonn, his father's home town, and excelled also in mathematics and engineering. He got a job with the International Railway Congress Association which seems to have paid him well, enabled him to travel widely, and left him generous scope for his interests outside railway engineering. The chief of these for many years was mountaineering.

He started climbing at the age of thirteen and was in the Alps with August Lorria in 1886. The year after that he went to North Wales and, with T. V. Scully, made the third route up Lliwedd, Central Gully and West Peak. The entry in the Locked Book says: 11th April 1887. Ascended the crags of Lliwedd by North face, first by central gully and next in line rather to the left of summit. Time $3^{1}/_{2}$ hours (under).' From then on Eckenstein was a frequent visitor to Snowdonia, climbing with most of the leading men of the time and exercising a powerful influence on the development of techniques and equipment. Many years afterwards Geoffrey Young recalled:

> Oscar Eckenstein, an engineer, with the build and beard of our first ancestry, was, I believe, the first mountaineer in this or any country to begin discussing holds, and the balance upon them, in a theory with illustrations. He had moved up with Frederick Gardiner from Pen-y-Gwryd to a shack at Pen-y-Pass, which he had fetched out of the Snowdon mines, and as I watched him hanging ape-like from the rock face of his eponymous boulder below the wall, and then passed my hand between his lightly-touching fingers and the rock it was the first suggestion of the balance and foot climbing later analysed in 'Mountain Craft'.

Although he climbed well and widely, in Mexico and the Himalayas as well as nearer home, Eckenstein's distinctive contribution was made not so much through his actual climbing as through his practical inventiveness. On the crags, he was generally content to take a supporting rather than a leading role. But on boulder problems or in the workshop, he turned his powerful and probing mind to fruitful considerations of all aspects of the sport. As Geoffrey Young pointed out, he was a pioneer, in theory and in practice, of the new art of balance climbing that was to replace the old thrutch-and-muscle methods. He invented and demonstrated the ten-point crampon. He designed the shorter ice-axe, light enough to be used easily in one hand. He made a close study of the rope and the comparative efficiency of various knots and was the first to insist that knots should always be tied 'with the lay of the rope'. He investigated the new tricouni nail and declared it 'worth further development and experiment'. And he pioneered hard living at high altitudes. In 1898, when Alpine gentlemen believed in spending the nights in the huts, he was found on the Schonbiel Glacier comfortably settled in a tent with a rubber underlay and a cork matress, using a nearby crevasse as his deep freeze.

His ideas were slow to find acceptance. Decades after he had demonstrated the labour-saving benefits of his crampons and shorter axe,

British Alpinists were still hacking their slow way across the great ice slopes in the traditional manner.

His influence would have been more acceptable, had he been a more congenial man. But he was neither genial nor congenial. It was not in his nature to compromise or temporize or suffer fools patiently. He had a fierce contempt for upper-class English attitudes and a special contempt for the way those attitudes dominated the Alpine Club. And he made no secret of it. Bluntly outspoken, devoid of humour or tact or charm, often offensive himself and always quick to take offence from others, it is hardly surprising that he failed to endear himself or his innovations to the Alpine traditionalists.

A natural Bohemian, scruffy and independent, he enjoyed the companionship of men of similar individuality. He climbed a good deal, for example, with Archer Thomson and there is no evidence of friction between them. And he climbed, in Britain and America and on K2 in the Himalayas, with a man who was even more, outrageously unconventional than himself, Aleister Crowley, and won from him an affectionate regard that almost amounted to idolatry. 'Eckenstein,' wrote Crowley in his *Confessions*, 'was the noblest man I have ever known. His integrity was absolute.' And he described Eckenstein's abilities as a mountaineer by contrasting them with his own:

> Eckenstein had all the civilised qualities and I had all the savage ones. He was a finished athlete; his right arm, in particular, was so strong that he had only to get a couple of fingers on to a sloping ledge of an overhanging rock above his head and he could draw himself slowly up by that alone until his right shoulder was well above those fingers. . . He was rather short and sturdily built. He did not know the meaning of the word 'fatigue'. He could endure the utmost hardship without turning a hair. He was absolutely reliable, either as leader or second man, and this quality was based upon profound and accurate calculations. He knew his limitations to a hair's breadth. I never saw him attempt anything beyond his powers; and I never knew him in want of anything from lack of foresight. . . In the actual technique of climbing, Eckenstein and I were still more complementary. It is impossible to imagine two methods

more opposed. His climbing was invariably clean, orderly and intelligible; mine can hardly be described as human. . . . His movements were a series, mine were continuous; he used definite muscles, I used my whole body.

It is impossible at this distance to form an assessment of Eckenstein's true ability because he despised all publicity and publicity-seeking. His notes in the hotel books are curt and factual, and many of them are concerned not with his own exploits but with refuting the claims of others. In the Locked Book, for instance, in January 1895, two men reported an ascent of Snowdon in difficult snow conditions. Eckenstein wrote underneath: 'Note. According to the statements of John Owen and of two gentlemen who watched this party and subsequently examined the tracks, the party went nowhere near the top of Snowdon. They did not even reach the top of the zig-zags. A mendacious account was published in "Black and White".' And in the Pen-y-Pass book, when someone challenged a point in a description of a climb in which he was involved but failed to sign it, he simply added the words: 'Anonymous criticisms are worthless. O.E.' (Plate 9)

For all his prickliness of temperament, however, and despite recurrent bouts of incapacitating asthma, Eckenstein was a regular and prominent player on the Snowdonia stage for many years. In July 1887 Corlett and Evans were in action again, this time on Cader Idris. An entry in the Pen-y-Gwryd visitors' book says: Ascended Cader Idris via the Arête of Cyfrwy—perhaps the finest in Wales. The Arête cannot be stuck to the whole way on account of a deep notch in it above which the rocks rise sheer.'

In the same year another cliff was introduced to the ways of the rock climber when Roderick Williams, a Liverpool solicitor, and his brother Tom climbed the South Gully on Tryfan. The following year they climbed Tryfan's North Gully, to emerge at the summit under the fascinated gaze of a young schoolboy called Geoffrey Winthrop Young. Young was twelve or thirteen at the time and was hill-walking with his father. Forty years later, in his book *On High Hills*, he recalled the moment:

Lliwedd.

Slanting Gully & W. Buttress.

Climbers generally are agreed that the easiest way up the cliffs of Lliwedd is the well-known Central gully & W. Buttress route.

The next easiest way, in my opinion, is a route symmetrical to the above. It may be described as the Slanting gully & W. Buttress route.

The route is up the Slanting Gully to the spot where the gully is divided by a projecting rib into 2 branches. The W branch is much the easier*

* [the statements in Menn R's book, p 25, are incorrect); the first few feet, which some may find awkward, are easily avoided by a short traverse from the E. — At the place where the 2 branches unite in easy horizontal traverse to the E leads to the ridge which forms the E boundary of the Slanting Gully. The way is then substantially along the edge of this ridge.

This route was taken on 26/9/06 by Messrs Bartmell, R & F Langford-James, & C. Smith & O. Eckenstein

A good climb but a little more difficult is obtained by continuing up the Slanting gully to the foot of the pitch below the cave. Here a crack runs up diagonally to the left to a higher point on the ridge mentioned above.

This route was taken on 25/9/06 by Messrs R & F Langford-James & O. Eckenstein.

* This is purely a matter of opinion, incorrect is not the word to use. ——

Anonymous ~~criticisms~~ collieries are worthless. O E

9. *Eckenstein in action in the Pen-y-Pass book.*

On the gallant top of Tryfan we saw two men emerge from the cliffs, roped together, the first sight of the rope! I believe this was in truth the occasion of the first ascent of the North Gully of Tryfan, and the beginning of modern rock climbing in Wales.

It was hardly, in fact, the beginning of modern rock climbing in Wales, nor was it, as Young was to claim elsewhere, the first use of the rope in Snowdonia. Wall and Stocker on Lliwedd had prior claims to both distinctions by more than five years. But the Williams brothers can be said to have introduced gully climbing to Snowdonia and to have earned the gratitude of all succeeding generations of rock climbers by first discovering the delights of Tryfan.

Their use of the rope was haphazard and rudimentary. A few years later Henry Gale Gotch came across Roderick Williams repeating the North Gully route with 'a party of five and carrying but 40 feet of rope amongst them (and therefore under the necessity of constantly roping and unroping)'. He was, however, impressed by Williams' ability: 'We were a little surprised to see Mr. Williams, after one or two attempts, scramble out of the Great Cave without a "bunk up".' Williams was a tall man and unusually agile. He seems to have done a good deal of pioneering lead climbing in the 1880s, but he is one of those who took no trouble to record his achievements so the details will never be known.

The inadequacy of the general use of the rope in those early days was tragically illustrated on Lliwedd on May 20th, 1888. According to, a full account in the Locked Book, Corlett, Evans and Kidson—all men of experience—planned to attempt the West Buttress, but found it so wet that they decided to wait for the rocks to dry. So they went for a long walk, via Crib Goch and Clogwyn y Person to the summit of Snowdon, and it was after five in the afternoon when they returned to the foot of Lliwedd. They decided to climb a route they already knew, the Central Gully, but there was still a lot of water coming down and they were fairly tired by this time. They only had a sixty-foot rope and, perhaps because they were in a hurry, they did not use it. Corlett led off, the rope slung over his shoulder, and reached 'a level portion about 300 feet above the screes'. Evans, following him, got stuck about eighty feet below Corlett's ledge. Corlett lowered the rope but it would not reach. He climbed down a little way but still it would not reach. Kidson had by now climbed up to Evans and helped him to a ledge. After a short rest he again tried to get up to Corlett but again failed. He returned to the ledge and shouted up, 'We are going down. I am clean fagged out.' So Corlett proceeded, alone, to the top, noticing, however, that the other two were still edging their way upwards

What happened next was seen from the screes and carefully recorded by E. J. Bedford in the Locked Book:

Kidson was sitting on a small sloping patch of grass. Evans seized Kidson's ankle and lowered himself to a rocky foothold a little further on. From this he grasped a ledge above affording an excellent handhold and worked his way towards the right. When he had gone about five or six feet—half the distance of the traverse—his feet slipped, his arms gradually came to their full stretch, and with one quickly uttered 'Oh' he fell. In four or five terrible leaps he fell over and over, a total distance of some 200 feet to the screes below. After once loosing his hold he did not appear to make any effort and beyond the first cry fell without a sound.

The fall occurred just before seven o'clock. By the time Kidson had climbed down to his friend 'life was already extinct'.

It was not the first death fall in the area. In 1861 a botanist and guide, William Williams, had been killed while looking for the Woodsia on the high slopes of Clogwyn y Garnedd. And in 1879 Maxwell Haseler wandered away from his party, a group of Birmingham walkers, on the Lliwedd ridge path and fell 600 feet or so to the screes. But these were fell-walking accidents. The death of Alfred Evans, at the age of twenty-four, was the first recorded rock climbing fatality in Snowdonia—the first of many.

The coroner's verdict was 'accidental death'. Haskett Smith's was: 'This accident need never have happened. If ever a party courted disaster it was done on this occasion.'

And in the Locked Book, E. J. Bedford wrote:

It is much to be regretted that the rope is not invariably employed in expeditions of this character. Had it been used on this particular occasion, in all human probability this terrible accident would not have occurred and a now sorrowing family would not be mourning the loss of one of its dearest members.

Chapter V

NEW MEN, NEW WORLDS

He revels in the sheer ascent in every grim recess.
And finds new worlds for wonderment
in every grim recess.

EIGHTEEN-eighty-nine saw the first appearance at Pen-y-Gwryd of two men who were to play major parts in the development of rock climbing in Snowdonia.

The first to arrive was A. W. Andrews, the son of a Wiltshire rector who had been a Scholar at Charterhouse and was now a Senior Exhibitioner at Magdalen College, Oxford. His rooms in college were immediately below those of the Rev. W. A. B. Coolidge, a Fellow of Magdalen and the leading authority on the Alps, who gave his undergraduate neighbour access to his unrivalled library of Alpine books. So the young Andrews, while reading classics, became fascinated by geography and mountain exploration. He was a natural athlete, good at soccer and an athletics Blue. A few years later he was to win the European championship in the mile, though he did it, by his own modest account, through 'an extraordinary piece of luck as there was a poor field through the failure of the best English runners to compete.' He was an outstanding tennis player too, competing regularly at Wimbledon in the years up to 1914 and reaching the semi-finals of the men's singles one year.

Andrews gave this account of his first visit to North Wales:

I bicycled across England and Wales to Pen-y-Gwryd, attracted by the rumour of novel rock climbing. I knew, to some extent, what to look for, as I had climbed on the Cornish cliffs and in Skye and had a limited experience of the Alps. . . . The veil of mystery was still hanging round the mountains of North Wales, and my hosts were not giving anything away to casual strangers. . . . So far as I knew, Lliwedd was in 1889 still entirely a virgin peak. I went up an easy slope to the left of the East Gully and then down the Terminal Ridge to the Terrace above the steeper part of the East Peak. I was alone and had no rope with me so that I did not go far down but saw enough to realise the possibilities. I then went on to the West Peak and scrambled down by what I feel certain was the Bilberry Terrace.

He also looked at the cliffs of Tryfan and the Glyders before returning to Oxford. But he cannot have felt greatly encouraged. He was neither the first nor the last young man to come up against the unhelpful obscurantism of some of the early habitués of Pen-y- Gwryd. It was to be twelve years before he returned, and by that time the climbing scene had been transformed through the impact of one man, James Merriman Archer Thomson.

'Oct. 27 1889. J. M. A. Thomson, M.A. Clare College, Cantab., and Bangor.' The note in the visitors' book is characteristically spare. There is no indication that he did any adventurous exploring on this, his first recorded visit. He had lived at Bangor, only a few miles away, for five years, without, it seems, paying any attention to the mountains. And several more years were to pass before he began his pioneer climbing.

Like Andrews, he was the son of a clergyman. Born in 1863, he spent part of his childhood in France, was then sent to Aldenham School, and won a Classics Exhibition to Clare College. Again like Andrews, he was a considerable sportsman, captain of the college soccer team and a member of the tennis team. He took his Classics Tripos and in 1884 went to Bangor on the coast of North Wales as a master at Friar's School.

The year after his Pen-y-Gwryd visit, he went to the Lake District and climbed Deep Ghyll on Scafell. In 1892 he repeated Roderick Williams' two gully routes on Tryfan and noted two possible variations in the Locked Book in his small, neat handwriting:

The South Gully of Tryfan. A detail. The steep rocks in the right-hand branch can be climbed straight up alongside the left wall. A grass patch is seen when looking up from below; this is the point to aim for.

The North Gully of Tryfan. A detail. The last pitch can be, in fact, climbed by getting on to the broad ledge beneath the jammed rock, thence on to the right wall—horizontal traverse of about 11 yards, then straight up. J.M.A.T.

But it was not until 1894 that he fell into the habit of making regular week-end excursions into the hills.

The early 1890s were a time of vigorous advance in the Lake District—the North Climb on Pillar Rock, Moss Ghyll on Scafell and Eagle's Nest Ridge Direct on Great Gable were all conquered in these years—but there was virtually no progress in Snowdonia. In 1891 W. E. Corlett had led his regular companion, M. K. Smith, up the Nor' Nor' Gully on Tryfan but this is an easier route than Williams' gullies. For the rest, there had been some activity but no achievement of note—until the arrival of Archer Thomson and two friends from Bangor, Henry Hughes and Henry Edwards. Many years later Henry Hughes, an architect by profession, gave a vivid picture of their early days of exploration in a talk to students:

At that time comparatively little rock climbing had been done in North Wales. Tryfan was beginning to be recognised as a fairly safe mountain for the beginner and learner. . . . The rock faces of the Glyders had never been climbed, nor had Twll Du, commonly known as the Devil's Kitchen. . . . In most of the early climbs I had the good fortune to be associated with Archer Thomson, afterwards a member of the Alpine Club, a most excellent all-round mountaineer, especially on rockfaces, without whose aid certainly many of the more dangerous climbs would not have been mastered. Another man who was closely connected with us in our climbs was Henry Edwards, then living in Bangor, whose dry humour relieved many a wearying experience. The number therefore as a rule consisted of three, a perfect number for rope work on a difficult climb. . . . Our general headquarters were either at Pen-y-Gwryd or at Ogwen Cottage, but sometimes at an out-of-the-way farm house, with an occasional visit farther afield as to Cader Idris. . . . Both Mrs. Owen at Pen-y-Gwryd and Mrs. Jones at Ogwen always most good-naturedly received and fed us if we turned up, no matter at what hour, even if they had retired for the night. In winter, if we could complete the difficult climb before dark, we were satisfied. We depended on a single folding lantern, lighted by a candle, to guide us down. On occasions naturally we got into difficulties. . . . There were no motors or buses in our days. We generally finished a day's climbing at Llanberis too late for the last train and, after supper at the hotel, walked the ten miles to Bangor. Or, finishing at Pen-y-Gwryd, had dinner there, and then started on the 18 or 19 miles walk back to Bangor.

All three of them were busy professional men. Their climbing was a Sunday pastime only. Nonetheless, in the first fifteen months of their partnership they put up at least fifteen new routes, ranging in difficulty from 'Easy' to 'Severe', on a variety of cliffs that included Lliwedd and Tryfan, the Glyders and Crib Goch, Braich Du and Clogwyn Du.

Perhaps the first outstanding climb they made was Central Gully on Glyder Fawr, a 700-foot route which the latest guide-book describes as 'Severe unless perfectly dry'. The date was November 25th, 1894. Eleven years later Thomson recounted the adventure with pedagogic humour:

We chose the Central or Blocked Gully, being deluded, as others have been since, by its relatively easy appearance. We began upon the (orographical) left wall, and have found since this route to be decidedly preferable to the actual bed, where a fine vegetation of lush grass has contrived to establish itself. Traversing back into the waterway, we soon reached a cave formed by a colossal block, spanning the entire width of the gully, to which it presents a smooth and vertical side. There being no exit from the interior, we were minded to have recourse to tactics hallowed by antiquity, and to form a testudo. Edwards and I leisurely discussed this plan and a precious flask of ginger ale, while Hughes, indifferent alike to malt and chaff, was absorbed in an endeavour, as it seemed to me, to pass a camel through a needle's eye, for he was trying to thrust a pliant rope up a long winding crevice discovered in the roof of the cave. However, half an hour later its appearance outside the chock-stone suggested an alternative solution to the problem. I am not concerned to discuss the propriety of this proceeding, for we were blissfully ignorant of the ethics of mountaineering, and it must have been due to an instinctive sense of morality that I protested while fastening myself to the rope-end with particular care and attention. I may add that on subsequent ascents respect for tradition has compelled me to adopt precisely the same contrivance. A free use was made of the rope up to the point of issue, which proved to be well below the top of the difficulty. There it was virtuously abandoned in favour of a good rock hold, much needed for the final struggle. The second man followed, while the third, to save delay, was brought over by an effective, but unceremonious, method, which happily left him too breathless to give vent to his feelings in words.

Not far above this cave we were confronted by a difficulty of a different character, the bed of the gully steepened into a wall coated with a layer of turf and matted grass, and this so loosened by the recent rains as to afford none but the most precarious foothold. We had begun to doubt the wisdom of proceeding further when the discovery of a crack underlying the soil near the right wall rekindled our smouldering hopes. Here it was necessary at each step to do pioneer's work with one hand while holding fast with the other, a process that would have become irksome, had not the leader been cheered by the thought that his companions were making light of greater discomforts, for, there being little freedom of movement, they were following, festooned with the dripping strips of vegetation which fell about their necks and shoulders.

Most of their first climbs, like those in the Lake District a decade earlier, were in the gullies. Just as mountaineers throughout history always looked for the easiest way to the summit at first, so rock climbers, confronting the steep cliffs, first sought to conquer them by way of the most obvious lines of weakness, the dark and broken gullies. They were not always, in fact, the easiest ways to the top, but their enclosing walls and short pitches and big ledges offered a psychological reassurance. For all their wetness, the slimy holds and sodden vegetation, they seemed safer. Increasingly, though, the pioneers discovered that some of the pitches they came to were too steep and holdless to be tackled direct. They were forced to look for ways round the difficulties by taking to the airy ridges and ribs at the side and, in this way, they found that more open climbing was possible and pleasurable too.

In May 1895 Thomson led Hughes, A. E. Elias and W. P. Elias, up the East Gully of Glyder Fawr. Next month he and Hughes conquered the East Gully of Glyder Fach which is still graded 'Severe'. The same summer found him venturing on to more open ground, with two routes on Glyder Fawr that are both graded 'Hard Very Difficult' today. One was Grey Rib, the other the West Gully which Thomson later pointed out is far from being what is usually expected in a gully climb:

> It might almost be termed a face climb, for the channel is shallow and does not quite reach the scree, moreover parts of it are too smooth to be climbed at all, yet the overhanging wall on one side and the great slabs on the other confine the climber to a very direct line. The first definite pitch at the top of a somewhat grassy incline proved a short ladder of wedged stones, and the second, which then came in sight, appeared an impassable barrier, for the right wall arches over and meets the precipitous slabs on the left. This face abounds in surprises for the explorer, and here, at a critical point in a breezy situation, I experienced the luxury of feeling given by the discovery of invisible holds when most required and least expected.

This weekly and increasingly bold activity by Archer Thomson and his friends marks the true beginning of rock climbing in North Wales. Before they came the sport was advancing in fits and starts and very cautiously. Now, in little over one year, the number of routes in Snowdonia had been more than doubled. The exploration of several new cliffs had begun. These men had clearly shown that regular climbing by a regular team, an adventurous leader with able support, could bring a dramatically quick extension in both skill and confidence.

These were the key years, chiefly by virtue of Archer Thomson's work but for another reason also—the arrival of some of the seasoned Lake District men. A few of them had already visited Snowdonia. Godfrey Solly had stayed at Pen-y-Gwryd in June 1890. A year later he brought a formidable team of Lake District and Alpine friends there—Norman Collie, Geoffrey Hastings and Horace Walker—but their only recorded expedition took them up Lliwedd by one of its already established routes on the West Buttress. At the end of May 1895, however, a more thrustful Lake District rock climber made his first appearance—Owen Glynne Jones, on the threshold of his brief but meteoric career.

Although he was a Londoner by birth and upbringing and although his climbing skills had begun and blossomed in the Lake District, Jones was Welsh by origin and had already done some exploratory scrambling on Cader Idris. He climbed the East Arête of Cyfrwy, solo, in 1888 and made first ascents of the East and the Great Gullies on Craig y Cau in 1894. But it was in 1895 that the mainstream of Welsh climbing felt the first impact of his remarkable personality.

He was twenty-seven years old, a science teacher at the City of London School, and a compulsive climber. From his first visit to Wasdale Head in 1890 he was captivated, climbing regularly in the Lake District during the Christmas and Easter holidays, in the Alps or the Dolomites in the summer. And when his work kept him in London he devised practice climbs on the inside and the outside of public buildings and monuments. Though slight of build and short of sight, he was phenomenally strong, especially in the arms, kept himself rigorously fit, and trained himself to endure and even enjoy great physical hardship. An anonymous writer in *The Climbers' Club Journal* of September 1900, describes him well:

> His attitude towards himself was precisely that of a marine engineer towards his engines. He quite admits that the machinery is high class, but his modest pride centres in the fact that he knows how to make the most of it, and can get more work out of it than any other man would. . . . The soul of mountaineering did not appeal to him so much as its physical charms. . . . Cold and wet seemed to stimulate him, and the worse the weather the better he climbed. . . . For

what is called 'style', he perhaps trusted rather too much to his unusually powerful grip; but, in all-round effectiveness, he had scarcely a superior among amateurs.

O. G. Jones went to Pen-y-Gwryd at Whitsun 1895 with a major objective in mind, the Devil's Kitchen, the dark, dank chasm that towers above Llyn Idwal. He believed it had never been climbed. He had planned to attempt it with Walter Parry Haskett Smith, but Haskett Smith did not turn up, so on May 31st, a showery day, Jones set off alone. He described his attempt in the pages of the Locked Book that evening. The first part went easily and at the foot of the Great Pitch, beneath the big chock stone, he scrambled up the little pinnacle to study the only possible way ahead, up the left-hand wall:

> The only available route up this wall starts from a small ledge and passes up a thin chimney that bears a little to the left. The first resting place is a grass patch, only large enough for one man, at about the level of the top of the pinnacle. Then the chimney bears rather to the right, and at a second small patch it becomes, in my opinion, impossible to ascend further. But from this patch a thin grassy traverse manifests itself towards the waterfall, and seems to indicate a route to the foot of the thin chimney to the left of the large jammed stone. . . . I divested myself of everything except shirt, knickers and stockings, and started up the chimney. Scarpetti would be just the thing for this kind of climbing, which approaches close in character to the wall climbing in the Dolomites. The chimney can only be used by the right leg and arm, the former frequently acting as a lever to keep the body, often overhanging, pressed against the wall. The holds are sometimes loose and falling stones much perplexed the writer and damaged his feet.

Jones had now reached the start of the rightward traverse. He was perhaps a little unnerved, partly by the forbidding gloom of the chasm—he was to have trouble here again—but chiefly by the unreliable nature of the rock. He studied the large block a few feet along the traverse and decided that 'it was likely to come away bodily'. It was, he judged, 'far too risky, with or without a rope'. He retreated, convinced 'that there could be no justification for a man continuing the ascent of the wall by himself, whether the weather were wet or dry'.

Jones had, in fact, been mistaken in believing the Devil's Kitchen had never been climbed. It had been done three months earlier, though as an ice climb not a rock climb. Immediately below his account in the Locked Book, a note says simply: 'Twll Du (the Devil's Kitchen) was climbed on March 2nd; the last part of the ascent was by means of the frozen waterfall on the right. JMAT. HH.'

Archer Thomson later gave a much fuller account of this ascent—perhaps the most remarkable and certainly the most famous of all his pathfinding exploits with Hughes in those crowded and creative months. He also amended the dating of the climb, by one day:

At 10 o'clock on March 3rd Hughes and I left Benglog Cottage, and striking a bee-line across Llyn Idwal, then sheeted with seven inches of ice, proceeded up slopes of snow towards the Devil's Kitchen; the surface crust was fairly strong, and only occasionally did we break through and flounder in the deep, soft snow beneath. Within the chasm the gradient increased gently, but the slope finally steepened to a severe angle, and the labour of ascent was materially augmented by the powdery condition of the snow which kept sliding from above with exasperating regularity, and obliterating our steps as soon as cut. The slope tapered to a chisel-edge, ending abruptly at the mouth of a semi-circular cavern; this was roofed with rock and floored with snow, slender pillarets of ice in welded clusters formed the walls, the whole structure appearing so fragile and delicate as to suggest almost a creation of the fancy—strange and beautiful. The cavern was some 25 feet deep from the roof; we fixed a rope to a planted axe and slithered down into it; the side we thus descended was a straight wall of snow and ice, against the outer side of which rested the slope we had previously ascended. The cavern occupied half the space between the walls of the Kitchen; outside it on the right stood a vertical bastion of ice, and this we hopefully began to attack. At first we could merely stand on the snow edge and deliver side-blows at the wall, for a large quantity of encrusted icicles had to be hewn away before it became possible to stand erect beneath and breast the obstacle. When a base of operations had been made we began to construct a series of steps easy of descent, by this means we were enabled to relieve one another, and endeavour to thaw in the relative warmth of the cavern where we found a welcome shelter from the wind which was constantly whirling the granular snow into columns and whisking its blinding grapeshot into our faces. Progress was inconceivably slow, for, as the right hand was always engaged in maintaining the balance, and there was no possibility of a body swing, the axe could not be used to advantage. According to tradition, our ancestor Thor was armed with a hammer for his battles with the Frost Giants, and with such a weapon we, too, were luckily provided in the form of a hatchet, surreptitiously removed from the worthy Mrs. Jones' coal-cellar at Ogwen. This implement proved of the utmost utility until the head took leave of the haft, and, glissading the snow slopes, vanished from sight. The head was recovered, and the hatchet, ingeniously repaired with string, continued to render us valuable service.

At two o'clock we discussed provisions in the cavern. Twelve ginger-biscuits and a morsel of chocolate was all we could muster between us, for we had anticipated an early return to Ogwen; yet, as this meagre meal was to suffice till eleven that night, it must be dignified by the name of lunch. Hughes renewed operations, and with so much added vigour that, half-an-hour later, he cut right through the ice wall, and I exchanged places with him to gain a view of the situation. The aperture was large enough to admit head and shoulders, and opened into a circular pit, two-thirds of the enclosing wall being of smooth ice and the remaining of sheer rock, down which a dribble of water trickled from above. It was about 10 feet in diameter, and stretched upwards some 20 feet from the place of puncture, and downwards perhaps 30 feet, but owing to darkness the bottom was not visible. The view was singularly impressive, and suggestive of grave possibilities in the event of a collapse. The presence of the pit was an unwelcome revelation; we had previously supposed the, ice to be solid to the rock, and as it was plain that we were engaged upon a giant icicle of questionable solidity, formed by the freezing of the water-fall, we reconsidered the situation, and sorrowfully concluded that it would be unwise to attempt further progress. It chanced, however, that the hatchet had been left at the hole, and, on going up to recover it, I fell almost mechanically to hewing at the ice above, and was encouraged by a little progress. Hughes then came under me, and with incredible patience held my foot for thirty-five minutes until I could advance to a small projection of ice festooned with icicles, which stood out from the main mass like a bracket from a wall. Hughes then retired to the cavern to act as sheet anchor in case of need, and here passed the time in elaborating many artistic designs, converting, as I afterwards learnt, the cavern into a comfortable boudoir, provided, too, with effective ventilation, for on striking the back wall of ice he broke into another chasm generally similar to that described above. My slow rate of progress was partly due to the impossibility of delivering very accurate blows with the hatchet, inasmuch as it was necessary to bow the head at the moment of impact in order to allow the detached fragments to fall thereon—at least, this plan was found by experience distinctly preferable to the alternative method of receiving them in the face. At length the wall gave way again; it was stronger than might be supposed from its thickness, here less than an inch, for it was ribbed and strengthened on the outside by icicles in bas-relief. The hole proved useful as a hand and foothold, and enabled me to reach sooner the level of a snow slope on the left, which hung over the entrance to the cavern, and from here I could reach with an axe to cut a step in it a foot above its abrupt termination. In the swing across the bearing powers of the step had to be taken on trust, and on such occasions few will not come nigh to momentarily envying the poet his 'foothold tenon'd and mortised in granite.'

The change to snow was very welcome; the slope, however, was abnormally steep, lying, as it did, on the outward face of the great wedged rock that dominates the pitch, the angle of which, according to an imperfect measurement is about 80 degrees. It was found expedient to hollow away the snow behind each step to avoid being tilted backwards by the bend of the knee in ascending. Thirteen feet above the gradient sensibly diminished, and the difficulties were at an end.

It was after seven when they completed the climb, already growing dark and bitterly cold. They decided to follow the longer but less dangerous path to Llanberis and reached the Dolbadarn Inn at 10.30pm, their clothes in tatters and one of Archer Thomson's hands so badly frost-bitten that he was unable to use it for several weeks.

Archer Thomson was to dominate the progress of Welsh climbing for the next decade and longer. He came to know many of its cliffs, and the intricacies of Lliwedd in particular, better than anyone else. When he climbed it was almost always as leader on the rope, and it was primarily his example that carried the sport out of the gullies and on to the ridges and buttresses where the holds were as small as the sense of exposure was great. 'He evolved,' Geoffrey Young was to write in 1913, 'the somewhat specialised type of climbing which has been principally responsible for the extraordinary advance made in the standard of difficulty during recent years; the slow controlled movement, depending on a fine balance rather than grip, and identical in pace and security upon easy crags or on the hardest passages.' *(Plate 10)*.

Thomson was a skilful and daring climber but also a very cautious one. He chose his companions carefully and would not climb with novices. He was punctilious about the nailing of his boots. He had no time for the technique, much practised by the Lake District men, of closely investigating a proposed new line by climbing down it with the protection of a top rope before venturing to climb up it without protection from above. Such a method, he said, was unfair; it imposed on the second party to attempt the route a harder task than had faced the first. He was prepared to spend a long time contemplating the next moves on a difficult pitch. 'Poised on nailholds high upon a steep slab,' wrote Geoffrey Young, 'he would lean right back from his waist, mutely meditating upon the difficulties above for minutes together.' And Haskett Smith said, 'He was like one of those great chess or billiard players who are never happy unless they can decide their play ten or twelve moves in advance.' Although he did much climbing in Wales and on Skye and in the Alps, he never had a serious fall.

10. Archer Thomson and Oscar Eckenstein looking for a route among Lliwedd's tangled and perplexing ways'. Geoffrey Young may have had this picture before him when he described Thomson '. . . leaning easily outwards, with half his body free, his feet and knees attached to the rock on some principle of balance all his own, and gazing upward with a smiling intentness that seemed half critical examination and half remote and contemplative pleasure.' (Photograph by A. W. Andrews.)

He was, in this respect and in almost every other, the antithesis of O. G. Jones. Jones relied on the strength of his arms rather than the delicate placing of his feet, on muscle rather than balance. Thomson's keen eyesight and careful observation made him an accomplished route-finder, while Jones, dangerously combining myopia with impatience, would hurl himself at the problem, trusting in his arms and his boldness to overcome the unconsidered difficulties, with the result that all too frequently he fell off. Jones' climbing was full of clatter and chatter, while Thomson was possibly the most taciturn man who ever climbed.

Stories about Thomson's capacity for silence have become legends. One man claimed to have spent a whole day on Snowdon with him without getting a word out of him. When they arrived back at Pen-y-

Pass in the evening, the man held out his hand and said 'Goodbye'. Thomson shook his hand, and smiled. On another occasion, it is said, he spent a day in the hills with a professor from Bangor University who had heard of Thomson's reputation and was determined to match it. They walked all day and neither said a word. But when they came to part that night, it was the professor who broke. 'I have a brother,' he said, 'who is even more silent than myself.' Thomson acknowledged the remark with a glance, but said nothing.

In a talk to the Alpine Club in 1918, Haskett Smith said:

> Never was there a man who felt more intense delight in the rocks than Archer Thomson; never was there one who displayed it less. Sometimes he would pass a whole day without uttering a word and even without changing the expression on his face. A Swiss who climbed with us once for half a day conceived an immense admiration for him and declared that he was more wonderful than the blind man who some years ago went up Mont Blanc. We were rather puzzled by the comparison till we realised that the speaker had never suspected Thomson of being anything but deaf and dumb.

Archer Thomson gave away nothing about his climbing or his feelings about it in conversation, and only a little more in his writings. He wrote many articles for *The Climbers' Club Journal* and the Club's first two guide-books, but it is only rarely that he gives a glimpse of his inner feelings. His writing style was factual and incisive and cool, sometimes witty and always idiosyncratic, showing a schoolmasterly taste for precision and erudite allusion. He meticulously avoided any hint of heroics. He was an intensely reserved and self-concealing man.

He might have lived longer had it been otherwise. Accelerated perhaps by greater professional responsibilities—he was promoted to be headmaster of Llandudno County School in 1896 —his introversion was to grow into a fatal neurosis. But that part of this story lies many years ahead. For the moment, in the mid-1890s and the years immediately following, Archer Thomson was the most consistently active and creative and venturesome climber in Snowdonia.

Chapter VI

THE GREAT GULLY PERIOD

Tighten the muscle, feel the strong blood flow
and set your foot upon the utmost crest.

THE last three years of the nineteenth century and the opening months of the new century saw considerable expansion and advance. Archer Thomson and his group continued their weekend visits, made new routes and discovered new crags, and began to devote more of their attention to the Snowdon area. Fresh recruits came in, among them W. R. Reade and Geoffrey Young. O. G. Jones brought his Lakeland friends, George and Ashley Abraham and J. W. Puttrell, on short but busy forays. In this period three major gully routes were finally conquered—the Slanting Gully on Lliwedd, the Devil's Kitchen, and the Great Gully on Craig yr Ysfa.

'It was the Easter of 1897 Owen Glynne Jones had elected to initiate my brother and myself into the charms of Welsh climbing, and we had spent a week of storm and sunshine on Cader Idris *(Plate 11)*. Then by way of Bettws-y-Coed we came to Pen-y-Gwryd, or P.Y.G. as the habitués are wont to call it, in a springless cart on a sunless day of swirling Snowdonian storm. . . . The hotel was well filled and, despite bad weather, the succeeding days went merrily enough.' The writer is George Abraham who was to become the leading exponent of the rollicking narrative school of climbing writers.

11. On the lower slopes of Cader Idris, Easter 1897. From left to right: Ashley Abraham, C. Fox, W. J. Williamson, O. G. Jones and George Abraham. (Photographer unknown.)

George and Ashley Abraham, heirs to a flourishing photography business in Keswick, had been drawn into serious rock climbing the year before by the irrepressible Jones. They had already become a formidable team with Jones as leader, George seconding and supporting him with advice and an occasional shoulder, and Ashley—the weightier though younger brother bringing up the rear and all the photographic gear. They had already done many classic Lakeland routes and some new ones. Now they had their sights on some of the Snowdonia 'plums', notably the Devil's Kitchen and Slanting Gully.

In the mid-1890s Slanting Gully seems to have loomed almost as challengingly in the minds of climbers as Cenotaph Corner on Dinas Cromlech did to the 'hard men' of half a century later. They were fascinated by it and afraid of it. They remembered the story of King Arthur's knights, still said to be lightly sleeping in their cave high up on Lliwedd. They knew that two strong but unidentified teams had attempted the climb and been driven back. They recalled particularly the fate of Mr J. Mitchell of Oxford, who tried to climb it alone on 30th August 1894, and fell to his death after standing for half an hour on the small holds just beneath the crux moves.

Jones had to leave the Pen-y-Gwryd party after a few days to keep a rendezvous with C Gully on the Screes above Wastwater. According to the brothers his parting words to them were, 'Whatever you do, leave the Slanting Gully alone!' The injunction was, of course, counter-productive *(Plate 12)*.

George Abraham was by now an able lead climber in his own right. Like Archer Thomson, he had been experimenting with the possibilities of balance climbing, relying on smooth movement and the careful, confident placing of nailed boots on small holds rather than brute force. On the morning of 27th April 1897, the brothers left the hotel saying they were just going 'to potter about, on Lliwedd'. When they returned that evening they were able to make a proud entry in the Locked Book:

> The western gully on Lliwedd, perhaps better known to climbers as 'The Slanting Gully', was climbed today by Messrs. G. D. and A. P. Abraham.

Later, George gave a much fuller account in his book *Mountain Adventures at Home and Abroad*. They made straight for their objective, dumped the camera equipment at the foot of the Gully, roped up and within thirty-five minutes they stood at the bottom of the pitch that had defeated all previous attempts:

> Roughly speaking, it was a deeply cut, eighty-foot crack, which started two or three feet wide and gradually narrowed to vanishing-point up above, where, when seen from lower down, it seemed to overhang ominously. On the left rose a great, smooth slab; on the right the rock construction was entirely different, spiky, undercut masses jutted downwards and formed a ragged-looking side to the crack. Unfortunately, these rocks seemed to have been laid the wrong way; could they have been turned the other end up, a kind of felstone

12. *A Pen-y-Gwryd group taken at Easter 1897, when the Abraham brothers were secretly planning their attempt on Lliwedd's Slanting Gully. From left to right, the people are: Back row: C. Fox, unknown, Rudolf Cyriax, unknown, Miss Buss and C. Legros. Middle row: Dr. Joseph Collier, Oscar Eckenstein, Mrs. Bryant, unknown, the Rev. Septimus Buss and A. D. Godley. In front: Miss Sophie Nicholls and unknown. (Photograph by the Abraham brothers.)*

staircase would have been available. The crack up which we had to climb seemed a species of fault between the two formations.

The lower part of the crack was smooth, and lubricated with slimy mud, so my brother steadied me up the left wall, whence it was soon possible to scramble on to a broad quartz ledge that ran across the slab on the left. The next few steps ahead looked smooth, so my henchman also came up to the quartz ledge. Suggestive marks and scratches on the slabs farther to the left inclined us to keep in the crack as far as possible. This plan may not have been the easiest, but it had the merits of safety, for the rope could be belayed around some firm rocks, which were wedged in the crack. A piece of the right wall protruded downwards in front, hiding the upper section and necessitating some awkward steps to the left on the exposed slabs. Then back I went to the friendly crack, where a mass of jammed splinters attracted attention. After careful testing, these were declared firm enough, so I undid the rope, threaded it up behind them, and re-tied the end round my waist. How strange no other parties should have noticed these splinters; they proved the key to success.

The views all round could not be appreciated in safety. The bend of the crack had brought us out above the huge slabs, which plunged gradually downwards. A small dislodged stone fell, not into the lower part of the 'cave,' but far down into the lower reaches of the gully, over 200 feet below. Glorious as was the scene from this aerial perch, with the gloomy lake of Llydaw nearly 1,000 feet below, the cloud wreathed shoulder of Snowdon 1,000 feet above, its full enjoyment was deferred.

My brother had meanwhile arrived at the wedged splinters, so, with parting instructions regarding the steady paying out of the rope, I launched into the unknown to taste to the full—

> 'The stern joy which warriors feel
> In foemen worthy of their steel.'

A step upwards and round a protruding section of the right wall revealed the final part of the crack. It was about 40 feet in height, smooth in structure, vertical at first, and slightly overhanging at the finish. Just for a moment there was a feeling of folly in farther advance, but 'courage mounteth with occasion'; once agrip with the intricacies of the ascent, all doubting thoughts vanished. Inch by inch, foot by foot, the rocks were overcome, trusty hobnailers bearing most of the strain, for strength of arm must be conserved against the strain of the final pull. At last this was reached with painful suddenness, for my head tested the solidity of the overhang. It was now advisable to gain a position of comfort, if the word may be applied to a human being hanging 'twixt earth and sky'. In looking around for the wherewithal to jam my body securely in the crack, my hand unwittingly touched an iron piton, which must have been very insecurely fixed, for it fell and went clattering downward to lodge on the quartz edge. Its presence immediately turned the thoughts to Mitchell's attempt. His farthest point had been reached. About a yard away to the left, on the exposed face of the slab, there was an unmistakable ledge which bore the traces of boot-nail scratches. The rocks below were scarred with long, straight, ugly marks as though of sliding boots. Instantly the thought came that the climber who deserted the crack for that exposed ledge would scarcely be able to regain his position, should upward progress prove impossible. An awkward bulge in the slab would prevent the return. Thoughts flash quickly at such moments: this was the rough theory quickly formulated on the spur of the moment as to the cause of the disaster. I see no reason now to alter it.

My only hope evidently lay in following the crack. The start was auspicious, for a partially wedged splinter left just sufficient room between its side and the wall of the crack for the thrust of a bony knee-joint. With this jammed in the crevice, all was firm, and the body could be raised until a small wrinkle was just available for the fingers of the left hand. The last stretch seemed now so near, that, with arms comparatively untired, there was a dangerous temptation to 'rush' the finish. This was the time to remember

> 'Who overcomes
> By force hath overcome but half his foe.'

The other half would certainly have been the victor on this occasion, for slow and deliberate movement, with right arm and leg doing the bulk of the work, showed a hopeless finish to the crack. Now came the call 'to stiffen the sinews, summon up the blood.' The last swing out on to the slab on the left tested the arms terribly, for the feet flew back into space; there was a strange sensation of emulating a fly crawling along a ceiling. Gravitation created an ugly backward pull until the body could be raised and steadied to a balance on a small foot-hold on the slab. Hereabouts several excrescences gave splendid help; the fingers gripped exultingly in a deep crevice behind some wedged boulders. The Slanting Gully was conquered.

The climb is today graded 'Hard Very Difficult'. The account shows that George was already aware of the advantages of balance climbing and skilful at securing his progress by threading the rope'. He believed that the piton he found—a rough wedge of iron with a hole at one end—dated from Mitchell's attempt but it seems more likely that it had been placed by one of the other unsuccessful parties to protect their retreat. At all events, when the brothers received a telegram from Jones announcing his conquest of C Gully, they were able to riposte with their own news.

The following day Ashley Abraham joined forces with Oscar Eckenstein and two young women, Sophie Nicholls and Sophie Bryant, to climb Lliwedd by the Central Gully and West Buttress Route *(Plate 13)*. It was the first ascent of the Lliwedd cliff 'by ladies', the first time, indeed, that women had figured at all in the story of Welsh climbing. But Miss Nicholls, at least, was a formidable climber. On this occasion she 'required no assistance whatever and acted as leader during more than half the ascent'. Two years later she became the first woman to lead Kern Knotts Crack in the Lake District.

The Abraham brothers now turned to the Devil's Kitchen—still awaiting its first ascent as a rock climb. They had read Jones' account of his defeat there two years before. They arranged to make the attempt with Eckenstein but, as he was late in arriving, they reconnoitred the final, crux pitch from above. Protected by a rope from Ashley, George inched his way along the traverse, reached the jutting rock that Jones had felt unwilling to trust himself to, and found it firm enough. Eckenstein had arrived by this time so they joined him at the foot of the climb, told him what they had done, and suggested that if he would lead them up the cracks already climbed by Jones, they would lead through and escort him across the traverse to complete the route. He agreed. Once again, George Abraham takes up the story:

> Our leader then advanced to the attack with my brother close behind him, whilst I coiled the rope around a knob of rock and belayed them as they climbed up the slippery, lower slabs. They soon gained the foot of the first crack which is about twenty-five feet in height, and with his right leg jammed in the crack Mr. Eckenstein

worked cautiously up it. I noticed that whenever he got beyond the reach of my brother's long arms he developed signs of discomfort and slid back to safety. This process was repeated several times. At last, when a piece of rock came suddenly away in our friend's hands at a dangerous moment, he made a precipitate retreat, and I clambered up to their level and tendered my sympathies.

Then, yielding to their persuasions, I tied on the rope and scrambled up into the beginning of the crack. It was not very difficult to climb this almost to the point where the first grass ledge could be reached, but at this place the risk seemed scarcely justifiable. Handholds were at vanishing point, and the only support was got by wriggling the right leg up the crack. This grew too narrow for this mode of progress just before I could grasp what was apparently a useful hand-hold on the ledge, and there was an unpleasant tendency for the law of gravitation to assert itself by pulling one over to the left.

This was an extremely dangerous situation, for the rocks were slippery and none too reliable. A collapse would have meant acquaintance with the top of the lower waterfall pitch about 100 feet directly below, so I followed the example of our leader and retreated down the crack.

So the Devil's Kitchen remained unconquered, though it had now been made clear that it would be done as soon as the right men and the right conditions came together. But this day's work—or, rather, George Abraham's account of it—was to cause trouble later.

The Abraham brothers were not made to feel altogether welcome at Pen-y-Gwryd. There was natural resentment that occasional visitors should manage to grab some of the choicer first ascents. This might have been more acceptable if their characters and approach to the sport had been more in the Snowdonia mould. But they were not like that. They were confident, straightforward men, not greatly given to cultural or intellectual reflection, and temperamentally incapable of the kind of diffidence and tact that might have been expected of newcomers. They tended to be rumbustious and even rowdy, full of high spirits and hearty jokes. On their first trip to Pen-y-Gwryd, for example, O.

13. *Climbers on the West Buttress of Lliwedd. The middle man is Eckenstein. Passing the rope hopefully round a notch of rock, as the top man is doing, was generally as far as they went in the way of belaying. (Photograph by the Abraham brothers.)*

G. Jones wanted, for some reason, to remain incognito and asked his friends to call him 'Faraday' when in company—which they loyally did until Mrs Bryant leant across the dining table one evening and said, 'Mr. Jones, why do your friends call you Faraday?' There may have been an element of snobbery in the hostility to them. They were 'in trade', shopkeepers as well as professional photographers, and they were bringing commercialism into climbing by selling pictures of climbers in action. They were spreading the word widely and their democratic attitude was sometimes seen as a threat to traditional exclusiveness. George Abraham referred to this in his book *Mountain Adventures at Home and Abroad*, in a passage about O. G. Jones: 'His favourite theory was that all men should climb, and that they would be the better for it. This was in contradistinction to the somewhat dog-in-the-manger idea which then prevailed, that the joys of the mountain were only for men of liberal education and of the higher walks of life.'

Whatever the reason—or reasons—for the Snowdonian hostility, there can be no doubt that it was there. In the introduction to their first book *Rock Climbing in North Wales*, the Abraham brothers, neither of whom was unduly sensitive or touchy, wrote:

> We have always found it most difficult to obtain accurate information regarding the newer climbs. The authorities, with a few notable exceptions, were very reticent and gave us but little practical encouragement. Often we have started out for a gully on the strength of an assurance that it was a well known climb, and almost as frequently have we encountered difficulties far beyond what were anticipated. In many cases these gullies had not even been visited.

By an odd irony, the man who befriended them on their first visit, Oscar Eckenstein, was the one who was to oppose them most fiercely in later years.

Another occasional visitor had other grounds for criticism. Professor E. A. Baker, one of the pioneers of Derbyshire grintstone climbing, reprimanded the North Wales regulars not for their élitism but for their idleness:

The torpids of Snowdonia took life much too easily. If there was a blizzard, or if rain fell in torrents, did they go out notwithstanding, merely to show that to an earnest mountaineer the state of the weather was a negligible trifle? Did they spend the time when they were not on the mountains performing strenuous feats on a billiard-table or going round a billiard-room cornice? Did they do finger-tip exercises and practise hair-breadth balancing on a stable wall or a neighbouring boulder? Alas, they did none of these bracing things. They shamelessly retired, when the weather was uncongenial, to the warmest recesses of their hotel and played bridge for hours on end.

The Snowdonia men would not have repudiated this charge com-pletely. They often confessed to lying in late in the morning—it made, after all, a pleasant contrast to the long and strenuous days of their Alpine summer seasons—and did not pretend that their evenings were always as boisterous as those at the Wastwater Hotel. But on the crags, in the closing years of the nineteenth century, the 'torpids of Snow-donia' considerably extended the range of their activities.

Archer Thomson was still in the lead. Until now most of his crea-tive climbing had taken place in the Ogwen district. Now he started to explore more thoroughly in the Snowdon area and particularly on Lliwedd. It was the beginning of a relationship between the man and the cliff that was to develop into a deep and lasting passion.

In April 1896, Thomson and his usual companions, Hughes and Edwards, joined forces with Eckenstein to open up a part of Lliwedd that had not been touched before. So far all the climbing had been in the area of the Central Gully and just to the right of it, on the West Buttress. Now Eckenstein indicated the possibilities of the East Gully and they set off to investigate. Thomson described how he reached

.... a species of roofless cave with a steeply sloping floor. From this cubicle there was no apparent exit. Eckenstein, who was separated by less than 30 feet, and had a long tail of rope trailing from his waist, joined me here to give me the benefit of his counsel and aid; pressing his back against one wall, and his feet against the other, he explained to me the exceptional security of his bridge-like position; it was one in which he could receive me in his embrace, if my attempt to climb out should prove abortive, and, as the next resting-place was obviously the heads of our companions below, I derived much courage and comfort from this assurance. The right wall is some ten feet high, straight and smooth; by utilising a crack in the corner, the climber is able to maintain his balance two feet above the floor; an unseen handhold above is thus brought within his reach, and a long draw-up lands him at the top of the difficulty.

This climb is called the Ordinary Route and graded 'Hard Difficult'. It was repeated by another party the next day, April 6th—an indication that things were now moving more quickly. At Whitsun the same year Thomson led the Craig yr Aderyn Route on the West Buttress of Lliwedd. And at Easter the following year, with Roderick Williams, he climbed the Elliptical Route which is still graded 'Just Severe'.

Thomson loved Lliwedd for its size and its intricacy. Its height and steepness gave him a thrilling sense of challenge and exposure; its complicated nature afforded an apparently endless variety of problems; it enabled him to exercise to the full his mountaineering qualities, especially his skill as a resourceful route-finder. But though his preoccupation with the complications of Lliwedd was a continuing one, it was never exclusive. He was a great discoverer of new cliffs for climbing. In March 1897 he made the first recorded route on Dinas Mot, which looks northwards across the Llanberis Pass. This was the Black Cleft, a 400-foot gully which is still graded 'Severe' and which was regarded for several years as the hardest climb in Wales. The next year, at Whitsun, he was a member of the large party which made the first ascent of Angular Chimney on the Gribin Facet above Ogwen. The climb was led by O. G. Jones—they were fellow-members by then of the newly formed Climbers' Club—but unfortunately neither of them left an account of this meeting of opposites. And two years later, at Easter 1900, Thomson worked out a number of variation routes on the Pillar of Elidr.

In the course of that same Easter holiday he made a more important find above Cwm Eigiau in the Carnedds—the cliffs of Craig yr Ysfa. 'They were discovered,' he wrote, 'in 1900 by three chance deserters from a picnic at Cwlyd, who revelled next day in the ascent of the deep cleft that cuts them from base to summit' *(Plate 15)*.

The party that made the first ascent of Craig yr Ysfa's Great Gully comprised Archer Thomson, R. I. Simey and W. G. Clay. They made the traditional leisurely, start from Capel Curig on the morning of 22nd April, took a long break for lunch, and did not rope up at the foot of the Gully until four in the afternoon. As a result, it was growing dark by the time they reached the hardest part of the climb, the Great Cave. Thomson described it as:

> . . . . . unquestionably the finest in any gully of the district. Rocks fallen from above and jammed between the vertical side-walls of the gully, form both the roof and two bridges. . . The removal of debris from these virgin pitches necessitated single climbing, with the result that strange gymnastics were indulged in here, before the top of the rock was reached, for the right wall was streaming at the time with cold water from the snow melting above, and daylight, moreover, had ceased to penetrate the recesses of the cave. The next move was across the bridge to a slippery ledge on the south wall; sidling along this string-course by the light of faith, we reached the outer bridge, where a hole afforded a convenient exit. A faint glimmer on the western horizon sufficed for the ascent of the little pitch above, and we reached the summit ridge soon after eight o'clock. Of the four hours spent in the gully, probably the major part was occupied in pioneering, for while the bed rock was found to be very sound and satisfactory, the obstacles were decorated with so exceptional quantity of loose turf and moss, that we might almost claim to have found them of grass and left them of granite.

He often returned to the Great Gully and always reckoned it 'the most entertaining gully climb in Snowdonia'.

Other men were opening up other areas. J. C. Morland took a party to Clogwyn du'r Arddu in December 1898—exactly a hundred years after Bingley and Williams' pioneer scramble up the East Terrace—

*14. Twll Du, better known as the 'Devil's Kitchen', rising above Cwm Idwal.
(Photograph bby Carl Rogers.)*

prospected both the terrace routes, East and West, but encountered ice-glazed rocks and, in his words, 'the leader declined to proceed'. T. K. Rose, a distinguished metallurgist who was later to be knighted for his work at the Royal Mint, made the first route on Idwal Slabs in August 1897 with C. C. B. Moss. This was the Ordinary Route which is not rated very seriously—Menlove Edwards described it as 'a route up the Slabs without having any of the difficulties proper to them'.

In this period, too, the Devil's Kitchen *(Plate 14)* finally capitulated to the rock climber. The victors were two young men from Blundell-sands in Lancashire, W. R. Reade and W. P. McCulloch, active pioneer climbers in the Lake District as well as North Wales but so much in the old self-effacing tradition that little is known of their achievements. Reade, however, is described by Geogrey Young as a tall lean man, a balance climber with an easy, composed style. The two men, who had made a close inspection of the gully some weeks before, took the train to Bangor on Saturday, 7th May 1898, hired a coach to Ogwen Cottage, and walked straight up to the foot of the chasm, arriving there at 6.15

in the evening. With characteristic modesty, their account of the climb, which was published in the first number of *The Climbers' Club Journal*, did not say who had led the final crux pitch:

At 6.25pm we attacked this crack. The leader, gripping one edge of it with his hands and knees, and obtaining extra assistance by jamming his right elbow and boot against the opposite side of the crack, squirmed up thirty feet of perpendicular rock to a small grass patch, where it is just possible for one man to stand. He then advanced by a similar method to another grass patch some twenty feet above, thus reaching the highest point hitherto attained by other climbers. Here it is hardly possible to stand without holding on, but he anchored himself in as firm a position as possible; and the second man followed, with the moral support of the rope, but had to stop in a rather insecure position some few feet lower down than the leader. To complete the climb, it was now necessary to traverse to the top of the waterfall, about sixty feet distant. The leader, finding some good hand-holds, started the traverse, but to do this he had to pass his legs outside the second man, whose head was on a level with the leader's knees. As soon as the leader was clear, the second man advanced to the grass plot, and, getting into a moderately firm position, waited until the leader reached a small projection of rock, eight to ten feet distant, which other climbers had thought loose. The passage took great care, as the foot-holds were poor, and the hand-holds had to be relied on almost entirely. On the leader reaching the projection, he hitched the rope over it, and the second man then joined him. The traverse after this became easier, the holds being good and well spaced, though most of them had to be cleared of grass and earth. Slowly advancing, one at a time, we eventually reached the cap-stone, at the top of the waterfall, and accomplished what is probably the first ascent of this remarkable chasm, except when two Bangor gentlemen cut their way up the frozen waterfall in the winter of 1895.

The climb from the slab to the cap-stone had taken us sixty-four minutes, and was rendered more difficult by rain, which had been falling for several hours.

15. George Abraham, on top, brings a companion up the pinnacle on Craig yr Ysfa. The man at the bottom is C. Fox. (Photograph by the Abraham brothers.)

Easter 1899 brought a second invasion by O. G. Jones and the Abraham brothers, who brought a large party of friends and relations including the grintstone pioneer, J. W. Puttrell, and a teaching and climbing colleague of Jones', F. W. Hill.

'We were a merry party at Ogwen that Easter of '99 [Plates 16 (a) and (b)],' wrote George Abraham, 'Mr. and Mrs. Hill and some cousins of Mr. Jones were staying at Capel Curig, and early each day, be the weather snowy, rainy or fine, their cycle bells were the first sounds to wake us in the morning.' The usual high-spirited practical joking took place. Jones instructed the Englishmen in some useful Welsh phrases and George promptly got into trouble for ordering 'roast baby' for his dinner. They had fun, too, with the Welsh name for the Devil's Kitchen, Twll Du: 'An ardent and affectionate pair, who had a curious knack of loitering to admire the view behind some of the great boulders, were credited with the version "Two'll do".'

But they also did plenty of climbing. A party of four was led up the Devil's Kitchen by Jones, who employed the technique of threading the rope behind blocked stones for added protection. In the Central Gully on Glyder Fawr this precaution proved its value. At the cave pitch Jones spent much time and effort pushing the rope up through a hole behind a blocked boulder. Finally successful, he tied on to the rope and began to climb, with George Abraham immediately below pulling in the slack as he ascended:

> Climbing up that icy rope proved extremely fatiguing, and just when our leader's feet were disappearing from my sight above the boulder, he gave a sudden call of warning. Almost at the same instant he came swinging down on to the rope and dangled helplessly in mid-air. Luckily the rope held firm; in fact, it wedged itself tightly in the hole. The situation was extremely exciting, especially for the spectators immediately below, but, after allaying their fears, I was just able to clutch hold of our leader's feet and pull him safely into the cave.

On Tryfan, Jones and the Abraham brothers pioneered the North Buttress climb and its Terrace Wall Variant. And on the crags of Clogwyn y Geifr, to the right of the Devil's Kitchen, Jones and George Abraham

16 (a) Ogwen Cottage in 1899. (Photograph by the Abraham brothers.)

Ogwen Lake Cottage.

JOHN E. JONES, Proprietor.

THE above Cottage, situated at the head of Llyn Ogwen—five miles from Bethesda Station, L. & N. W. Railway—is the chief centre for climbers visiting Snowdonia.

Twenty minutes walk from the famous Llyn Idwal, and within sight of Tryfan, Glyders Fawr and Fach, Carnedd Dafydd, and other principal mountains of the Snowdon group.

The Cottage is on the high road, and conveyances meet visitors at Bethesda Station if so desired.

Every comfort and accommodation at moderate charges.

Tariff on Application.

Letters should be addressed—
" Ogwen Lake Cottage," Bethesda, North Wales.

16 (b) Advertisement for Ogwen Cottage in the Climbers' Club Journal of 1904.

devised two new and slimy routes, Hanging Garden Gully and what they called the Devil's Staircase.

It was the last day of their holiday—their companions had already departed—when they set of early in the morning for the foot of the Staircase. They failed to find a way up the first, most difficult pitch so they scrambled along the traverse from the Devil's Kitchen to join the Staircase cleft above the difficult part. Jones led off, using George's shoulder as a foothold at one point, and shortly reached the foot of the final pitch. There, in George's words,

. . . . a small sloping ledge just afforded us enough accommodation to survey the work ahead. This proved to be a veritable chimney, for a black hole led upwards, apparently into the heart of the mountain; and we christened the place the Devil's Drainpipe. I was left on the narrow ledge whilst the leader crawled up into its dark recesses, and the sounds of his progress gradually faded into the distance, until I heard a call from the open air some fifty feet above my head. At the same moment there was an ominous rumble in the Drainpipe! It took but a second to realise that a rock was descending its dark interior, and there seemed every probability that it would sweep me off the small ledge on which I stood. It was a helpless feeling, but the suspense was soon over for the rock whizzed out of the dark hole, and before the real danger could be appreciated, it had scratched some skin off my left ear, and gone crashing down the cliff to the bottom of the gully.

They completed the climb. 'In the midst of our success,' George wrote, 'we little thought, as we took off the rope and revelled in the warm May sunshine that our last climb together was over. Plans and arrangements for a visit to the far distant Himalayas the following Christmas had formed the bulk of our leisure conversation, but fate decreed it otherwise.'

On 28th August, O.G. Jones was killed in the Alps when one of his guides slipped and fell from the West Arête of the Dent Blanche.

Chapter VII

THE CLIMBERS' CLUB

We held the heights for life's brief minute;
For us the crags and cwms loom there:
This is our Club, with good friends in it . . .

THE Climbers' Club was conceived in 1897 and born in 1898. It was not the first club to be formed for British mountaineers and climbers. The Alpine Club, concerning itself almost exclusively with the exploration of the high mountains of Europe and further afield, had been in existence for more than forty years; and in the last decade two more groups had come formally together to meet the needs of home climbers in particular regions, the Scottish Mountaineering Club and the Yorkshire Ramblers. The Climbers' Club was, however, the first attempt to unite British rock climbers. The prospectus which was circulated in March 1898 to invite applications for membership stated: 'The object of the Club will be to encourage mountaineering, particularly in England, Wales and Ireland, and to serve as a bond of union amongst all lovers of mountain climbing.' In the event it only partially succeeded in this aim. The years that followed its formation saw the birth of more clubs of strictly regional interests—the Kyndwr Club for the Peak District, the Fell and Rock for the Lake District—and decades were to pass before anything like a national association for all British climbers was achieved. The Climbers' Club remained primarily, though not entirely, the club for men who climbed in North Wales. It was an inevitable result, perhaps, of the circumstances of its creation. For it evolved naturally and directly from the Society of Welsh Rabbits and the Pen-y-Gwryd Hotel.

In that congenial atmosphere, where conventionalities were not obtrusive, and the bishop and the man of law shared the sofa with the old shepherd and deferred to his opinions, men of various sorts, but united in their deep love of the mountains grew to know each other; and their sense of association, the germ of the Club, struck its first root.

The words are those of George B. Bryant, who played a leading part in the formation of the club and, as its first secretary, in nursing it through its early years. Haskett Smith later paid a characteristic tribute to Bryant's powers of organization and persuasion: 'With him it was not Bryant and May but Bryant and Must.'

According to Bryant's account in the first issue of the Club Journal, it began as a purely social affair. On 19th May 1897,'about 40 frequenters of the Welsh farmhouse' gathered for a reunion dinner at the Café Monico in London to talk over old times. Their chairman was T. S. Halliday who had succeeded C. E. Mathews as the moving spirit of the Welsh Rabbits. The idea of some form of 'Pen-y-Gwryd Club' was mooted at this dinner, and when they met to dine together at the same place seven months later Roderick Williams formally proposed the motion 'That a Climbing Club should be formed'. It was seconded by H. G. Gotch and passed unanimously. The Rev. J. N. Burrows, who was in the chair on this occasion, then proposed that C. E. Mathews should be asked to become their first President, and this was 'cordially acclaimed'. A nine-man provisional committee was chosen to draft the circular and get the venture under way.

The circular was posted in the spring of 1898. It stated the aims of the Club, suggested an annual meeting and dinner in London, and proposed an annual subscription of half a guinea. They expected up to a hundred applications for membership. They got two hundred.

On 28th April 1898, sixty-two members of the Climbers' Club—the name had been decided by then—assembled at the Alpine Club rooms in Savile Row for their first annual general meeting. They elected an impressive committee, which reflected the national nature of their intentions. It included R. A. Robertson, President of the Scottish Mountaineering Club; Cecil Slingsby, one of the leading Alpinists who had eagerly taken to British rock climbing; the leaders of successive generations of Lake District development, Haskett Smith and O. G. Jones; and several Snowdonia men, including Roderick Williams, H. G. Gotch and E. R. Kidson. Bryant was to be the Club Secretary, T. K. Rose its Treasurer.

After rejecting a proposal that the annual subscription should be raised to one guinea, they adjourned to the Café Monico where their number increased to eighty for the first annual dinner.

In the manner of those more expansive times, at a charge of 7s. 6d. a head, they had:

Hors d'oeuvres varies

Consomme Marie Louise
Creme Chantilly

Saumon a la Richmond

Eperlans Colbert

Mousse de jambon, sauce supreme
Selle d'agneau aux petits pois nouveaux
Canetons d'Aylesbury—Salade
Asperges d'Argenteuil, sauce Maltaise
Pudding d'Orleans

Glace a la Monaco—Petits fours
Laitance sur canape

Dessert

Then the President proposed the toast 'Our Club'.

C. E. Mathews was an experienced after-dinner speaker. He had been President of the Alpine Club. His appointment to the presidency of the new club had inspired Douglas Freshfield, one of the Alpine Club men who made no secret of his contempt for the new breed of rock-climbing 'gymnasts', to light verse:

Why is it to the Alpine Club?
Our C.E.M. no longer keeps?
Why should he found—himself as hub—
A Climbers' Club for' chimney sweeps'?
The answer, Sir, is very clear clear:
To give elsewhere those famous speeches
That flow—impromptu?—year by year
From your epergne of grapes and peaches!

Mathews replied effectively in his speech: 'There is magnificent hill-climbing in the British Isles. I retain as vivid impressions of Great End, of Lliwedd and of Tryfan as I do of the Dent Blanche or the South side of the Matterhorn. The memories of Wastdale or of Pen-y-Gwryd are quite as enduring as those of Chamonix or of Zermatt. At last our mountaineering ladder is complete, and the youth of England can be reassured. They can matriculate at the Climbers' Club, they can graduate in the Alps, and can carry off the highest honours in the far-off regions of the Caucasus and the Himalaya.'

He went on to note, with satisfaction, the nature of the new club's composition. One third of its founder members were members of the Alpine Club too, 'a good and healthy sign'. There were contingents from the two senior universities, both dons and undergraduates. There were representatives of many professions, lawyers and solicitors, authors and journalists, clergymen and civil servants, merchants and manufacturers and inspectors of schools. 'Some of us,' he said, 'know what hard work is in the various occupations of our lives. We must have some alternative, and we are all agreed that there is no alternative comparable to mountaineering. It is a sport which combines admirable physical exercise with pleasures of a purely intellectual kind. It is a sport which makes us young again . . . . It is a sport which brings us face to face with Nature, and puts us in quest of the unknown. . . . It is a sport which enables us to throw off the cares and troubles of life. . . . It is a sport that from some mysterious cause appeals mainly to the cultivated intellect. 'Arry or 'Arriet would never climb a hill. . . . Above all, it is a sport that makes a man. It teaches boldness, prudence, co-operation, self-control.'

Fifty years later Geoffrey Young was to write in praise of the Club's tradition of after-dinner oratory: 'It has been marked by the courage with which the speakers, and especially the Presidents, have let themselves go: they have dared to be eloquent and even dramatic, in description and citation.' It was Mathews who launched this tradition and maintained it for the first few years of the Club's life. His themes remained constant. 'How is it,' he wondered at the second annual dinner, 'that of all sports it is mountaineering that appeals to the cultivated intellect?' And if his reference to "Arry and 'Arriet' rings rather too bluntly on modern, more socially sensitive ears, it had at least the merit of truth. For the fact is there were no working-class rock climbers in those days or for many years to come. The membership of the Climbers' Club was drawn from the ranks of the comparatively affluent, the professional upper middle class. Some of the intellects, of course, were more 'cultivated' than others but they were, without exception, men of good education and half of them at least were university men. And they fully represented the British rock-climbing community of this time, south of the Scottish border: the Abraham brothers and Godfrey Solly from the Lake District; Puttrell and Baker from the Peak District; Baumgartner and Bowring, a Vice-President, to represent the mid-century days of pioneer fell-scrambling; Frederick Gardiner and Frederick Morshead to speak for the Alpine interest; and almost all the men who had contributed to the development of Snowdonia climbing, including Archer Thomson and Eckenstein.

It was decided, ambitiously, to issue a quarterly journal at a cost of one shilling. Its first editor was E. R. Turner and his first edition contained Bryant's account of the formation of the Club, a full report of the first general meeting and dinner, the list of members, and descriptions of two recent first ascents—the Abraham brothers in Slanting Gully and Reade and McCulloch in the Devil's Kitchen.

In its first summer the Club organized two climbing meets, at Wasdale Head and Pen-y-Gwryd, and in the second number of the *Journal*, which came out in November, an anonymous writer reflected on the lessons learnt: 'The majority of climbers appear to prefer trying some well-known gully or face to striking out new routes for themselves. That this should be the case in the Cumbrian hills is scarcely surprising; indeed, there, where every chasm has received a name, and every needle and pillar is, figuratively speaking, dotted with routes, it is difficult for anyone who is not an expert to make a first ascent. Many of our finest rock climbers have devoted themselves to the district for years, and anything that has successfully resisted their constant attention may be reckoned extremely severe. But it is not so in Wales. The Cambrian hills have not undergone the systematic examination that has been accorded to their English rivals, and even on Snowdon itself there are numerous gullies about which little or nothing is known. A striking example of this is Clogwyn du'r Arddu. . . . If this precipice were situated within easy walking distance of Wasdale Head, it would probably have a literature of its own; but as it is, it suffers from an ill-deserved neglect and is comparatively unknown.' The writer also complained of the Snowdonian secretiveness that had troubled the Abraham brothers and was to persist: 'The frequenters of Pen-y-Gwryd have a strange aversion to putting their experiences into writing. Many of them resolutely decline to make even the shortest entry in the special book provided at the inn for the purpose; and although persistent inquiries will sometimes result in a verbal description being given, all efforts to obtain a detailed account are usually futile.'

Over the years the *Journal* did much to break down this reticence. Its editors—A. W. Andrews took over from Turner in 1904—succeeded in bringing out a fresh edition every three months until the end of 1910. Their approach was catholic. They gave the Club's news, reports on new climbs, reflective articles on the sport in general and occasional pieces of wider interest, geological, botanical and literary. They offered plain prose and poetic prose, poetry and pictures. The chief, continuing interest was the advance of the sport in Snowdonia and Archer Thomson was persuaded to produce accounts of his discoveries, but the *Journal* also recorded developments in Cornwall and Northumberland, the Alps and the West Indies, Mexico and Skye. It reflected, too, a serious concern for conservation. The second edition welcomed the news that a scheme for a light railway between Portmadoc and Beddgelert had been turned down, then went on: 'The steam tramway from Llanberis to the summit of Y Wyddfa, unsightly though it is, has served one good purpose. It has concentrated the ordinary tourist and excursionist upon the least interesting side, and left rock climbing in undisturbed possession of the wilder portions of the mountain. Were it not for this fact, the ever-increasing hordes that over-run Snowdon during the summer months would compel the climber to desert it and seek less frequented cliffs. Only those who have attended the ascent of one of the Clog-y-Garnedd gullies on a fine August or September afternoon can quite appreciate what a source of danger the great British tourist is. As Mr. Pilkington says "No amount of climbing skill or precaution will save you from a well-aimed ginger-beer bottle."' And in September 1901 the *Journal* was reporting on a railway threat to the Vale of Gwynant and printing an appeal from Canon Rawnsley for money to help the National Trust buy a mile of the western shore of Derwentwater.

In the manner of such things, the literary standard of the *Journal* was far from consistent but at its best it was very good indeed. It printed, for example, Mathews' 'Reminiscences of Pen-y-Gwryd' and A. D. Godley's delightful poem, 'Ode on a Very Distant Prospect', which became a popular anthology piece. It introduced to print two of the outstanding writers of later years, Geoffrey Young and Aldous Huxley. And one issue, that of 1912, must still rank as possibly the best club journal ever produced. By that time it had become an annual production, costing three shillings and edited by Arnold Lunn. The number covered the brilliant 1911 Alpine season; it had Geoffrey Young on 'Climbing Down', Archer Thomson on Llechog and Eckenstein on 'Claws and Icecraft'; it dealt with climbing developments in South Africa and the Pyrenees, Etna and the British sea cliffs, Ireland and Northumberland; E. W. Steeple recounted his first ascent of the Grooved Arête route on Tryfan and Hugh Rose Pope reported on the state of the sport at Wasdale Head; there were considered pieces on mountain writing and mountain painting; and much else, including Hilton Young's witty 'Counterblast to the Perpendicular'. Two years later, the last *Journal* before the war presented George Mallory's famous article, 'The Mountaineer as Artist'.

Unhappily, the Climbers' Club came into being at a time when the home of its origin, Pen-y-Gwryd, had entered upon a period of disturbance and decline. Harry Owen was dead. His widow Ann struggled to keep the place going with the help of her granddaughters but the loyalty of the 'Welsh Rabbits' must have come at times under testing strain. One of them later recalled, in the club *Journal*: 'Dear old Mrs. Owen had grown too feeble to maintain the old style of homely farmhouse comfort, and no modern improvements had taken its place. . . . Dirt and discomfort reigned supreme. All the food had a strong flavour of rust and mould, and the beds were not merely damp but actually wet. The windows of the bedroom would neither open nor shut, and one of the walls was adorned with a mass of solid ice fully five feet long. Even the Aiguille du Midi hut, when the floor was entirely covered with ice, was not so damp.'

Mrs Owen died in 1896 and was buried beside her husband in Beddgelert churchyard.

By the summer of 1901 the Pen-y-Gwryd was up for sale. Adjacent notes in the Club *Journal* for June that year tell the story:

We learn that Pen-y-Gwryd Hotel has been put up for auction, but has failed to find a purchaser. An offer of £950 was received, but a reserve of £1,460 having been fixed (for goodwill and furniture) the property was withdrawn.

Gorphwysfa. The enlargement of the hotel at Pen-y-Pass is now nearly completed, and by the time the autumn season commences the new licensee, Miss Pritchard, expects to be able to offer accommodation to all the regular frequenters of Snowdon. *[Plates 17 (a) and (b).]*

Miss Pritchard forged ahead. She had learned her trade at the Dolbadarn Hotel in Llanberis. She was soon advertising her renovated hotel at Pen-y-Pass as 'the most convenient centre for climbing on Snowdon and the Glyders. Coaches from Llanberis, Beddgelert, Capel Curig or Bettws-y-Coed stations if desired.'

In 1903 she married Rawson Owen, a local man though no relation to Harry Owen. He was a regular soldier, who had fought with the

17 (a). *The hotel at Pen-y-Pass in 1895, a few years before it became the great centre for climbers. (Photograph by Rudolf Cyriax.)*

Y Gorphwysfa.

(Late Pen-y-Pass Hotel.)

Mrs. OWEN - - Proprietor.

THE above Hotel, situated at the head of the famous Pass of Llanberis, the finest mountain defile in Wales, is the most convenient centre for climbing on Snowdon and the Glyders. Coaches from Llanberis, Beddgelert, Capel Curig, and Bettws-y-Coed daily from May to September.

Conveyances can be sent to Llanberis or Bettws-y-Coed Stations if desired.

Tariff on Application.

Letters should be addressed—
Y Gorphwysfa Hotel, Llanberis, Carnarvon, D.S.O.

17 (b). *An advertisement for Y Gorphwysfa in 'The Climbers' Club Journal' of 1904.*

14th King's Hussars in the Boer War. He got his discharge from the army in 1906 and joined his wife to make the Pen-y-Pass Hotel at the crest of the Llanberis Pass the focal point for the rock climbing community.

So P.Y.P. on P.Y.G. succeeds,
Owen on Owen.

Geoffrey Young was quick to see the advantages of Pen-y-Pass :

The temptation to the mountaineer proved invincible. The highest roosting-place in the island—and a luxurious one at that—where he was lodged upon the rim of space, and spared the twenty minutes' extra road-trudging at morning and evening. . . . With its "beds and its brass", its artistic furniture and good cuisine, and, later, with its electric lighting and increasing supplies of hot bath-water, Gorphwysfa became a place of note. Rocks can be wet and cold in Wales; and home cheer, warmth and a careful dryingroom are matters of consideration in arranging that a large mountain party shall retain its cheerfulness through all the familiar weather changes.

It was the ideal place for the development of his famous Pen-y-Pass parties.

More than half a century later, in his book *Mountains with a Difference*, Young recalled his first glimpse of Pen-y-Pass:

On the first walk through North Wales with my father and elder brother, we came out of the great dark Snowdon chasm over the ridge of summits under Crib Goch. As I was pushing ahead in thick mist, among ghostly crags, a cold gust blew a gap in the cloud under me, and I was looking down and down, over a desolation of precipice, to where one sunray shone upon a patch of grey and white cottage at the head of the remote Llanberis Pass. The glimpse made a consoling human contrast with the immense surroundings of descending columnar crag and scar; and it has stayed vivid in memory, even when the cottage later grew into familiar Pen-y-Pass, and the misted nearer summits became the favourite walk of my later, and limited, years.

Chapter VIII

GEOFFREY YOUNG

Joy comes: joy of our kindred sense and sight,
joy of the oneness quick in all moving things;
in the soundless fall of leaf, in the swift's shrill wings,
in the pulse that throbs from man to the infinite.

G EOFFREY Winthrop Young has a secure place in the history of mountaineering. In the ten years up to the start of the First World War he was the key man, both as climber and as moving spirit, in the advance of rock climbing in North Wales. But this is only one, and by no means the most important, of his claims to fame. In terms of climbing, his achievement in the Alps was the more impressive. As a writer about mountaineering, in prose and poetry, he had no equal in his time and has hardly been surpassed for evocative power. He was a close analyst of the sport, too, and the first man to study its physical and psychological demands in depth. He was a great mentor and year after year his enthusiasm and charm brought promising young men to British rock climbing and Alpine mountaineering. And, remarkably, after he had lost a leg in the War, his influence and inspiration grew even stronger. To an unusual degree he combined a deeply mystical approach to the sport he loved with a cool and rational appreciation of the way it was developing. When he became President of the Alpine Club in the Second World War he used the weight of that office and his great personal authority to fulfil his long-cherished ambition to create a united voice for British climbing interests. He set in train the work that led, in 1944, to the creation of the British Mountaineering Council. There is probably no one to whom English-speaking climbers owe a greater debt of gratitude.

His achievement was astonishing, but it is also true that he had every natural advantage. He was born in 1876, the second son of a third baronet. His home background was comfortable and cultured and liberal in its sympathies. He had an alert intelligence, an easy aptitude with words and considerable social charm. He grew up strong and compact in body and outstandingly good-looking.

The path to the hills was made easy for him. His father, Sir George Young of Cookham; had been an Alpine man in the 'Golden Age' when British gentlemen and their European guides conquered every major summit in the Alps. He had taken part in the first ascent of the Jungfrau from Wengen. The year after that, 1866, one of his brothers was killed when they were descending Mont Blanc, guideless, and Sir George did no more serious climbing. But he still turned to the hills for relaxation and it was on hard walking holidays in Wales that the young Geoffrey felt the first stirrings of what was to become a lifelong passion.

He went to school at Marlborough. According to his own account, he was browsing through the Sixth Form library one day when he took down a copy of Whymper's *Scrambles in the Alps:*

> With the first reading the horizon shifted. Peaks and skies and great spaces of adventure rolled upward and outward, smashing the walls of a small, eager, self-centred world. . . . Snows and glaciers began to 'haunt me like a passion'; the delight in the thought of them always tempered by a little ache of unsatisfied longing. . . . In our school hymn-books we, of the choir at least, were accustomed to scribble the date over the hymn of the day and add the record of any great event, such as our appearance in a school match or the winning of a school prize. It is curious now to read among these scrawls the first assertions of a new personality, less arrogant, or, at all events, less priggish: 'Shall I ever go to the Alps?' and 'If I could only be a mountaineer!'

He knew Snowdonia well by now and the hills of Kerry and Wicklow and Killarney. But it was not until he was between school and his first term at Trinity College, Cambridge, that he became a rock climber of sorts: 'Looking back, it seems very proper that my own first rock climbs should have been on the Fells, where rock climbing in this country began. They were made with contemporaries who had caught something of the enthusiasm, and knew even less than I did about the matter. I made a very frightening one-man ascent of the Napes Needle in thick mist to begin with; and my first use of the rope—a hay rope borrowed from Mrs. Wilson of Watendlath—involved myself and Richard Feetham, later the heroic and saintly Bishop of North Queensland, in a tangle of incompetence on the West wall of the Pillar Rock and a hair-raising new line of descent never afterwards identifiable.'

Once established at Trinity he went to the Lake District regularly with reading parties of university friends and developed his skill on Borrowdale volcanic rock. He liked to travel up on the overnight train—to heighten the contrast between his busy undergraduate life and his mountain holidays—and alighted at Keswick station early one morning to be hailed by 'a genial, red-whiskered man in rough tweeds, with the words "Hullo, young man, oughtn't you and I to talk?—nailed boots go straight to my heart."'

This was John Wilson Robinson, one of the founding fathers of the sport. It was a nicely symbolic encounter, a coming together of the two pioneering generations of rock climbing with much in common and much, too, in contrast. For Robinson was the complete Lake District man, a farmer and a formidable fell-walker and a climber of tireless enthusiasm. He hardly climbed anywhere else. He went once to the Alps but was not impressed and never wanted to go again. His climbing, like his character, was whole-hearted and uncomplicated. But Geoffrey Young had already set his heart on bigger mountains of snow and ice as well as rock, and his mind was already contemplating the effects on a man's innermost being of long and testing days in the hills, 'the pulse that throbs from man to the infinite'.

At Cambridge he studied Classics for his degree, read widely in literature and history, and won the Chancellor's Medal for English Verse two years running. He made many friends. And he kept his muscles in climbing trim by exploring the college roofs at night. The result was his first published work, *The Roof-Climbers' Guide to Trinity*. It was done as a Rag Week joke but it was done thoroughly, carefully researched and heavily larded with learned quotations in parody of the mandarin style of some of the early Alpine guide books. 'In these athletic days,' he said in the introduction, 'of rapid devolution to the Simian practices of our ancestors, climbing of all kinds is naturally assuming an ever more prominent position.' He had found himself 'forced to seek new sensations on the artificial erections of man'.

The book lists six main routes, gives detailed descriptions of them, and takes passing notice of what it calls 'Wayside Problems', the roof climber's substitute for bouldering. Route A, for example, is summarized in these words: 'New Court. Complete Circuit; time, 45–60 minutes; guide superfluous, but rope necessary; expense, repair of pipes and possible doctor's fees.' And the description of the route includes this passage: 'The turrets may divert our efforts for a moment, but in deference to the slumbering don it is best to pass rapidly round a convenient ledge on the inside of the crenellations, which removes the necessity of clattering over the roof.' His account of Route B, the complete circuit of Cloister Court, notes: 'It is possible to gain this point by a most interesting little cross-route from the gyp-room window of a certain famous first-floor historian.' The historian was Lord Acton.

Young's fellow-explorers included George Trevelyan, destined to be a famous historian himself, and Sandy Mackay who later became a judge. Their climbing involved a lot of combined operations—climbing up and over each other. Because its legality was uncertain, they had to climb in darkness and, as far as possible, in silence.

The publication of Young's *jeu d'esprit* meant the college authorities could no longer ignore the extra- and super-mural activities of their students. In 1901 the Vice-Master of Trinity told the College Council to investigate the matter and determine whether roof climbing should be allowed. A Committee of Inquiry was set up which included—to their great delight—George Trevelyan and Geoffrey Young who had both gone down from the university by this time. 'It was great fun,' Young recorded. 'We climbed everything in full daylight with two of the porters carrying the fire ropes behind us, in procession! As a result of the report, the sport was made—officially—illegal!'

Predictably, this merely gave an added *frisson* to the practice. Roof climbing continued in Cambridge and spread to Oxford where an 'Alpine Club' was formed to explore the fabric of 'the other place'. Very soon afterwards the Great Gate of Trinity, one of the problems that had defied Young and his friends, was climbed by a notorious eccentric, Horace de Vere Cole.

In 1905 Young produced another spoof 'slim volume'. This was entitled *Wall and Roof Climbing* and parodied the academic manner of the time by bringing an enormous weight of apparent scholarship to bear on the history of the sport. It made subtle distinctions between the problems raised by climbing on brick or stone, cement or iron, monasteries or mosques. It even dealt, in a series of appendices, with the separate characteristics of haystack climbing, tree climbing and what was called 'Interior Climbing'—on and around doorways, tables, chairs and staircases.

It was during his time at Trinity that Young attained his schoolboy ambition and began to climb in the Alps. In 1897 he was in the Tarentaise region and in the following two seasons he visited the Valais and the Oberland and started to undertake serious routes, including the Viereselsgrat on the Dent Blanche and the Grand Cornier which he climbed solo.

He left Cambridge in 1900 *(Plate 18)* and went to Eton to teach German and General Subjects. One of his pupils, L. E. Jones, later recalled his 'ardent and distinguished mind and Renaissance good looks . . . He was grave and impersonal . . . . I never remember him speaking of himself or saying a word irrelevant to the matter in hand.' He made no attempt, apparently, to interest the boys in mountaineering. Indeed, they had no idea that he was already an Alpinist of great promise.

The long school holidays enabled him to develop his Alpine experience and extend his acquaintance with the hills of Britain. In the summer of 1903 he made a cycling and walking tour in County Donegal with some Irish cousins, and on the way home visited Cecil Slingsby's

18. Geoffrey Young at about the time he left university.

family at Carleton in Yorkshire. 'Delightful family and pretty children,' he noted in his diary—his first reference to Slingsby's daughter Eleanor who was seven years old at the time and who was to become his wife sixteen years later. Then he went on to Pen-y-Pass to join George Trevelyan and Page Dickinson, one of his Irish cousins, and one or two other friends. On this first, embryonic Pen-y-Pass party, they achieved little. His diary recorded: 'Too cold and stormy but climbed on Y Wyddfa, North and South Gullies of Tryfan. Parson's Nose.'

The time was ripe for Snowdonia to take the lead. Rock climbing had been forging ahead in the Lake District for a generation. At Whitsun, 1903, Fred Botterill crowned the achievement with the first ascent of his eponymous slab on Scafell. But in September that year four young men fell to their deaths from the face of Scafell Pinnacle. It was the first fatal accident in twenty-one years of increasingly adventurous climbing in Cumbria, and it had a traumatic effect. For several years the advance of the sport in the Lake District was almost at a standstill. In Snowdonia, on the other hand, everything was set for a period of rapid development. Archer Thomson and his friends were still very active and new men were coming in. In 1902 H. B. Buckle and Guy Barlow had made the first ascent of the Gashed Crag route on Tryfan, which was probably Geoffrey Young's first serious rock route in Wales. The hotel at Pen-y-Pass, under new management, was becoming the new focal point. Oscar Eckenstein had led the move up the hill by acquiring an old iron shed, the relic of one of Snowdon's recurrent mining failures, and setting it up near to the hotel as 'a Bohemian redoubt'. From now until the outbreak of the First World War the sport's main centre of advance would lie in North Wales and particularly in the talented group that gathered around Geoffrey Young.

The atmosphere of the period is brilliantly captured in his writing. He told the story many times, never more vividly, perhaps, than in the opening chapter of *Mountains with a Difference*:

> Climbing then had the freshness of a dawn. Nobody was on the hills but the few farmers and herds and ourselves. Outside the initiate circle, no one bothered about us. The cliffs lay round us unvisited, with their mystery of 'climbs'. For those first years we sped over

fells and hills alone or with the few, realising the glory of untrodden height and of the movement and effort its steepness demanded. I came down at evening generally with reluctance, because rest and reaction, sensations delightful in proportion to the greatness of the effort which leads on to them, were even better enjoyed among the heights themselves. Only once again in life, when returning slowly to strength remade all over in bone and nerve after the wounds and long fever of the first war, have I felt that sense of a new awakening: of a return to the dewy morning of life when man first became conscious of himself and of the achievement opening out before him.

And in the opening paragraph of the chapter he evokes the special delight of making a first ascent:

On the first of the new rock climbs which I made in North Wales, a climb up a square-cut chimney at the southern end of the Glydyr Vach precipice, I looked down the grey falls of scree on to the wide green Nant Francon valley with its thin riband of winding road, and I thrilled suddenly with a new feeling. For hundreds and thousands of years, high and close above the passing and repassing of countless generations, this upright corner of beautiful and solid England— or rather Wales—had been waiting unvisited, untrodden, even unseen, until, during the few days of my own short life, the climbing enthusiasm had broken over us, and had set me, miraculously, upon it. Here upon this ledge since earth took form out of chaos no one before me had set foot. On that glister of crystal quartz under my hand no eye before mine had ever rested. I tingled as I stood, to the very bootnails. And an enchantment as secret and enthralling as first love seemed opening behind and within all the unvisited cliffs and mountain walls in my sight.

Young's literary style is highly charged and deeply personal, alive with insights and bright pictures, infused with the delight he found in climbing and the companionship of the hills and the company of friends. It is serious and yet full of joy, careful in phrasing yet emotional and romantic in content—over-romantic at times, perhaps, for modern tastes. For the would-be historian of the period he is infuriatingly vague about facts; he rarely gives the date and often omits the precise location. But he was concerned to convey something more important than mere fact, to re-create the spirit and feeling of the time, and in this his success was complete.

It is thanks to Young's books and articles that we have so full and lively a picture of the Pen-y-Pass community, with pen-sketches of its leading figures. The one portrait he does not give, except between the lines, is his self-portrait *(Plate 19)*. This omission was partially rectified by Robert Graves who was introduced to Pen-y-Pass in the spring of 1914 by one of his masters at Charterhouse, George Mallory. In his classic autobiography *Goodbye to All That,* Graves speaks of Young's caution as a climber:

It appeared not merely in his preparations for an ascent—the careful examination strand by strand of the Alpine rope, the attention to his boot-nails, and the balanced loading of his rucksack—but also in his caution on the rock-face. Before making any move he thought it out foot by foot, as though it were a chess problem. If the next handhold happened to be just a little out of his reach, or the next foothold seemed at all precarious, he would stop to think of a safe way round the difficulty. George used sometimes to grow impatient, but Geoffrey refused to be hurried. His shortness put him at a disadvantage in the matter of reach. Though not as double-jointed and prehensile as Porter, or as magnificent as George, he was the perfect climber; and still remains so.

Young's attitude to mountaineering and his facility with words led him naturally to poetry. He became a master of light verse and enlivened Climbers' Club dinners with pungent and ingeniously punning rhymes. He turned his hand to serious poetry too. His first volume, *Wind and Hill,* was published in 1905; the next, *Freedom,* in 1914. The mood is that of Wordsworth's 'emotion recollected in tranquillity', controlled but passionate. His continuing theme is nature, and especially mountains, and the effect of close contact with nature on the developing mind. He was not a major poet—he lacked Wordsworth's ability to astonish the reader with lines of reverberating power—but the body of

19. *Young and Charles Trevelyan (on the right) were co-founders of the Man Hunt on the Fells which still takes place annually from Seatoller in the Lake District. They are wearing the red sashes which denote that they are the 'hares'. This photograph was taken just before the First World War.*

his verse, published in a collected form in 1936, represents the biggest and the best assembly of mountain poems in the language. And some of the poems recapture the feelings of the rock climber more tellingly, perhaps, than any other writer has succeeded in doing.

His best-known lines, most quoted and most frequently anthologized, are those of '*The Cragsman*':

> In this short span
> between my finger-tips on the smooth edge
> and these tense feet cramped to the crystal ledge
> I hold the life of man.
>
> Consciously I embrace
> arched from the mountain rock on which I stand
> to the firm limit of my lifted hand
> the front of time and space:
> > For what is there in all the world for me
> > but what I know and see?
> > And what remains of all I see and know,
> > if I let go?

Geoffrey Young was born in the heyday of Victorian confidence and this was reflected in his character, in his relish for life, the breadth of his interests and the whole-heartedness with which he pursued them. He was a man of vigour, physical and intellectual, and a lover of good company. He liked to share his enthusiasms. He was a considerate and sensitive friend. One of his protégés, Claude Elliott, said many years later, 'You felt he had an insight into your thoughts and reactions.'

His manner did not impress everybody equally. There were some, particularly in the post-war years when his features grew more magnificently leonine and he came to be even more lionized, who thought his circle was too élitist and Young himself too grand-mannered. There was, it was said, a strong streak of the actor in him, the poseur even. He could be curt and dismissive and was capable of flashes of outspoken anger especially when he detected sloppiness in thinking or climbing. Mallory himself was on the receiving end of fierce rebukes for over-hasty climbing on more than one occasion. Young's standards of

20. *Young in the 1920s.*

conduct were high and he expected his friends to live up to them as rigorously as he did.

Unlike many of the elder statesmen figures in British mountaineering in the first half of this century, Young was no blinkered reactionary. In the two fields of his greatest interest, education and mountaineering, he took the enlightened, liberal view. He knew there was no point in blank resistance to change, and if the changes that came were not always to his liking he was prepared to bring all his powers of persuasion and patience to the task of modifying them.

Fundamentally, although he could adapt and develop, he did not change. 'I climbed all my life,' he wrote, 'for enjoyment, and abandoned myself to it.' But the enjoyment was not superficial, the abandonment was not wild but controlled and self-aware. He loved climbing for the balm and the freedom it gave his spirit and for another, almost sensuous reason:

> There was never a pleasure in life to me like watching well-timed movement, in dancing, jumping, running climbing, walking. As I travelled, I saw people in their movement, and unconsciously classed them by its right or its ill adjustment. I enjoyed as greatly the feeling of rhythm and appropriate motion in myself. The glory of the high dive through air, meeting the water on the right curve for a noiseless surface-rush, the exultant passage from parade to lunge in fencing, the swerving run that took me over the line at Rugby football, the leap from any moving vehicle with the triumphant sway in balance as one met the ground, the continuous balancing of the body in motion above the dead-stop footholds taken on steep ice or rock, above all, the entrancing rhythms of the waltz absorbing all conscious movements into a dreaming pattern of sound—these were the positive pleasures of life in passing.

For Geoffrey Young these were the good motives for mountaineering and he was not prepared to compromise them when the post-War expansion of the sport brought new forces into play *(Plate 18)*. He criticized those who turned climbing into 'a scientific study or skill, measured by grades of difficulty and exposure, by exhaustion and by sensations which, if I have interpreted many modern mountain books rightly, have little of pleasure among them.' He derided in verse the

> . . . long grey valleys of technique
> Where the dry bones of dead sport wait us,
> Graphs, formulae and apparatus.

And he despised men who climbed for personal or national glory. Climbing was a passion for him, but never a fanatical obsession. And when he discovered, after years of painful struggle to resume his Alpine climbing with an artificial leg, that the effort outweighed the pleasure he gave up climbing and took again to hill walking.

Chapter IX

THE PEN-Y-PASS COMMUNITY

Come home mountain friends, to your Rest on the Pass,
Come back, mountain climber, to me.

GEOFFREY Young left his teaching job at Eton in the summer of 1905 and became an inspector of Schools for the Board of Education, traveling widely from his base in Lincolnshire. His formative climbing in these years took place in the Alps but he contrived one or two brief visits to North Wales each year, sharing his time between Ogwen Cottage and Pen-y-Pass. It was not until Easter 1907 that he inaugurated the tradition of the Pen-y-Pass parties *(Plate 21)*. His diary records:

Arranged for a large party at Pen-y-Pass and Pen-y-Gwryd and crossed England from Gainsborough in the car.... Picked up Marcus Heywood at Stockport and then to Chester, Mold and Flint. Then, in a lilac and gold sunset all along the coast road of North Wales, to Caernarvon in the dark. . . . At Caernarvon met H. V. Reade and next day up to Pen-y-Pass. Took Marcus up Lliwedd and then made two new ascents of the East Buttress with H. V. Reade and Andrews. Later the crowd came including Captain Farrar, Eckenstein, Archer Thomson etc. A delightful crowd. My car joined up the two hotels and all made me welcome. Climbed the great Craig yr Ysfa Gully and led my rope. Also the Slanting Gully, the Horned Crag route,

21. Group at Pen-y-Pass, 1907. From left to right they are: Standing: O. K. Williamson, unknown, Marcus Heywood, Geoffrey Young, Percy Farrar. Sitting, middle row: W. R. Reade, Geoffrey Bartrum, George Mallory. Sitting, front row: E. B. Harris, F. Don, F. Sparrow, Oscar Eckenstein. Extreme right: J. M. Archer Thomson. *(Photograph by A. W. Andrews.)*

Cyrn Las and thoroughly explored the East Buttress. Had a search party round to Ogwen in the dark for three incompetents. A glorious time! Ran down to Portmadoc in car, enthusing Page Dickinson with the scenery.

Here was the nucleus of the community. Herbert Reade and his wife were to become vital elements. He was a small, meticulous man, a senior civil servant. Mrs Reade became the social organizer, a plain woman but possessed of formidable charm and, on occasion, devastating wit. Page Dickinson was to recruit the Irish contingent which gave a light-hearted leavening to the later parties. The old Snowdonia guard was fully represented, while Captain Farrar—famous for his strong language—was already a leading Alpine authority. He had seventeen Alpine seasons behind him as well as climbing in Canada and Japan and distinguished service in the South African War for which he was awarded the D.S.O. Young later described him as '. . . a typically British figure, soldierly, distinguished, straight-backed, abrupt, with all the prejudices as also the virtues of its type, with the rough humour, the impulsive initiative, the essential dignity.'

Another Boer War veteran was permanently at Pen-y-Pass by this time—Rawson Owen the landlord. While his wife supervised the hotel itself, he was happy to demonstrate his horsemanship by driving the climbers to their chosen crag in 'the smartest pair and brake in Wales', enlivening the journey with fanciful accounts of his service in Africa.

The exploration of Lliwedd was already, as it was to remain, the chief activity. Recent years had produced a number of new routes, most notably the Horned Crag—pioneered by Archer Thomson and Eckenstein—and A. W. Andrews' solo conquest of Slanting Gully and Slanting Wall. Now, in 1907, eight new routes were added to the list. Two of them, Shallow Gully and the Roof Route, were the work of Geoffrey Young and Herbert Reade. Five of them were Archer Thomson's.

It was during that summer that Thomson began his intensive investigation of Lliwedd. In September, with E. S. Reynolds, he made two particularly impressive new climbs—the first Girdle Traverse of the crag, climbing across all four buttresses at about mid-height, and what he called the Avalanche Route. In an account for *The Climbers' Club Journal* Thomson explained why he chose the name:

Between Route 1 and what is now called the Central Chimney Route a deep chimney about 8o feet in height was found, cutting the wall above the scree. An opening is given by this chimney which affords by its a position a proper, and by its steepness, an appropriate introduction to the climb which lies above. At one point an obstruction forces the climber out on to the left wall, but he can first hitch his rope over a useful spike. A few yards west of its exit the mountain throws down the gauntlet in the form of a massive rib. When Reynolds, who had joined me, had obtained anchorage to his liking,

I scrambled over the prominent corner, and was disappointed to find the view curtained off by a subsidiary rib. There were, however, just sufficient holds to permit what seemed to be a traverse to Nowhere. Once round the second corner, Utopia appeared in the shape of an elementary ledge on a wide expanse of exposed slabs. On reaching this I was glad to find a belaying-pin for the rope, of which some sixty feet had not run out. My companion was delayed, I believe, by some rearrangement of the rucksack, but the indistinct sounds that reached me gave the impression that more rope was needed. I therefore descended to a spot where I could hold the rope on a knob with one hand and at the same time sit on a sloping wrinkle. The interval was not dull. To light a pipe with the free hand proved a lengthy task of absorbing interest. This done, the air around suddenly vibrated; I was pleasantly fanned by a flutter, accompanied by a tremulous booming closely resembling the low notes of an organ. Nothing was visible and the noise slowly subsided and ceased . . .

The cause was plain when a crash was heard and a great boulder and numerous satellites were seen chasing each other down the scree directly below. My shouts elicited no response, neither were they audible to my companion round the rib, but they startled an innocent wanderer a mile away on Crib Goch who repeated them in order and with needless verbal accuracy to the company assembled in the evening. It was then learnt that a party of three young climbers were at the time finishing their ascent on the Terminal Arête.

Thomson's developing delight in balance climbing is illustrated a little later in the same article:

The nook is one of those from which each newcomer must necessarily evict the man already established, so, having no alternative, I exchanged the seat in the eyrie for a stance on the belaying-bitt. From this aerial spot the view was unique. I seemed to be standing on a vertebra of the backbone of the mountain. An impossible crag rose directly above, and smooth slabs shelving away on either side presented an outline of delicately undulating curves. This romantic environment produces on the mind an impression of isolation at a great height.

I stepped from my perch to the rocks on the right, and rounding a corner, encountered a vertically fluted wall. The position thereon was extraordinarily exposed, for there stretched below 300 feet of open face which betrayed no trace of ledge or furrow. By stepping warily in and out of the shallow grooves I found it possible to work upwards on small holds in a slightly oblique line, and within fifty feet of the bollard I chanced upon a knob of rock which enabled me once more to hitch the rope.

The issue hardly remained any longer in doubt. The climb began to change in character, and we were soon approaching at a quickened pace the level of the Cairn Traverse, almost embarrassed by the choice of good things provided here by nature for the support of man.

The other great Lliwedd expert, A. W. Andrews, was also at work. Geography was his profession—he was a university extension lecturer—and exploration was his hobby, in the Alps, on the Cornish sea cliffs and in North Wales. He was equally happy climbing alone or in company, up or down or across the cliffs. 'I happened to be a little weak in the lift of the leg in climbing,' he wrote, 'and had developed fingers and arms inordinately to monkey-standard, so that many climbs came easily to me which other climbers found difficult. I also specialised in going down and have, I think, climbed down nearly every climb I have been up.' He often accompanied Archer Thomson though they never made a new route together, but his usual companion was the great botanist, Professor (later Sir John) Bretland Farmer: 'I was very lucky in having Farmer as a climbing companion. He was an exceptional rock climber, with a long reach and very sound knowledge of the structure of rocks and especially clever in avoiding unsound holds.' They made several routes on Lliwedd together—Central Gully and East Peak in 1906, the Bowling Green-Central Gully Connection the following year, and the Central Chimney Route in 1908.

Like several of the early Snowdonia men, Andrews had a talent for light verse and many years later he used the form to pose a question:

> Who was it raised rebellion first and went
> One step beyond the immemorial law,
> And freed us from the bonds of precedent
> Which fixed the footgear that all climbers wore?

The answer, though he does not make the claim in the poem, was Andrews himself. He was the first man to climb the rock routes of Snowdonia in rubbers, 'in tennis shoes, the soles being as thin as possible to help the feel of the rock'. Sometimes he persuaded his companions for the day to do the same but it was to be a long time before rubber soles became generally accepted. Andrews wrote: 'I remember Thomson standing outside Pen-y-Pass before starting off for the day and, while putting in tricounis or nails on worn leather boots, watching our footgear. But he never made any comment.'

Geoffrey Young and his friends were at Pen-y-Pass again for Easter 1908 and, despite bad weather, climbed on Lliwedd, Craig yr Ysfa and Crib Goch Buttress. The party tradition was established and the gatherings became regular, always at Easter, often at Christmas too. Twenty years later Young wrote:

> .... we used to meet at this time once or twice in the course of each winter, a company of men, women and even children, of diverse ages and interests. The mountain atmosphere provided a common inspiration excellent for social purposes. Our ideas and our muscles alike were kept agreeably on the stretch; and for a few days a very perfect society reminiscent of the conditions of the golden age fused itself out of our individual oddities. Once again, and by chance, we made the familiar discovery that the activity of the body, properly developed and guided, could interpret as effectively as any speech or writing such graces as might exist in the mind. At the same time the clash of wits, the sympathetic criticism felt but unspoken, and the mutual understanding which must emerge in any entirely natural society serve to modify each original egoism, maintained a right balance between elements too exclusively intellectual or too enthusiastically athletic, and kept every chance assembly casual, unselfconscious and light-hearted.

When they were there they took the place over. There would be as many as sixty of them crowded into the hotel and the Eckenstein shack and a scattering of tents. Young controlled the invitations and organized the daily excursions, seeing that each party was sensibly composed and no one's abilities were over-stretched. Mrs. Reade looked after the women and children in the party—their inclusion in such numbers was unprecedented in British mountaineering—and ensured that everyone had a good time in the evenings without offending the proprieties.

Unfortunately, Young's writings form not only the chief, but almost the only source of information. He cannot be claimed as an impartial witness. Even so, there can be no doubt that these meetings at Pen-y-Pass were both fruitful and enjoyable. The climbing was serious but they would return each evening to their 'Rest on the Pass'—roast joints were the speciality—and to varied and lively company.

Like their Lakeland predecessors at the Wastwater Hotel, they devised indoor contests of suppleness and strength. H. O. Jones, a brilliant Cambridge scientist, was there in 1908 and recorded their achievements in an intriguing, if rather baffling, entry in his diary:

Pushing penny along floor.	L. Noon	
. . . measured from toe.	W. Owen	
Holding on rope with both hands	C. J. Nash	70 seconds
Kicking match box.		
Kicking leg on floor in front of other	HOJ	3' 1½"
Pushing penny between legs		2¼
Lifting up on foot	3' 2"	HOJ

There was a battered piano and to its accompaniment they sang verses of their own composition. Young writes:

The long evenings of impromptu songs and varied entertainment were alternated, as whim dictated, with gymnastic feats in the hall; when the casual visitor might enter to find Eckenstein hanging upside down by his hands on a rope; H. O. Jones, or Miss Bronwen

Jones, kicking over the matchbox with incomparable finesse; Leslie Shadbolt, Harold Porter or Miss Sanders (later Lady O'Malley) swinging easily up on to the window-sill; the children, in confederacy, perpetrating some general joke upon the company; or Owen himself performing his great feat of climbing round the chair-back—a *geste* which in twenty-five years no other succeeded in repeating. And the parodies, the poems and imaginary 'Chronicles'! They were composed during climbs or walks in the day, and delivered to the smoking-room floor—whereon the majority sat—the same night. Tradition dictated that they should not be preserved; the spirit of confident youth and hope decided that there must and would be always new ones.

A handful of these effusions were, in fact, preserved. Among them was Herbert Reade's advice to the young climber, sung to 'The Aesthete's tune from *Patience:*

> If you're anxious for to shine in the mountaineering line
> > as a man of prowess rare,
> You must build a firm foundation on a mass of information
> > and your intellect prepare.

And another was said to have been composed by Trevenen and Julian Huxley to mark the occasion when they spent a miserable winter night in a cave near the Parson's Nose and reached Pen-y-Pass next morning to find the place empty—everyone else was out looking for them. The chorus of their song was:

> > So never be a search party,
> > But stay at home in bed,
> > Or the lost ones you are seeking,
> > Will eat breakfast in your stead.

They have been derided by a later generation as 'elegant evenings' but they were hardly that. Dress was informal and generally scruffy. A good deal was drunk, usually beer, and the air would be heavy with tobacco smoke. Mrs Reade puffed away at endless cigarettes and most of the older men were addicted to pipes. Eckenstein's tobacco—Rutter's

Mitcham shag—was the most noxious of all. There were party games and songs and, most of all, conversation. Mountaineering must have been the general theme of their talk—stories and reminiscences, discussion of the 'ethics' of publication, arguments about the course of climbs on 'Lliwedd's tangled and perplexing ways'—but they were men of widely ranging interests and their conversation was often at a very high and general level. A few years earlier C. E. Mathews had wondered why the sport was so attractive to 'the cultivated intellect'. Had he lived to enjoy the Pen-y-Pass parties—he died in 1905 —his wonder would have grown. It would be difficult to find any other sport, at any period of its history, whose members could claim a comparable average I.Q.

The three Huxley brothers, Trevenen, Julian and Aldous, grandsons of the Professor Huxley who had climbed Snowdon in December 1860, were passing through Eton and Oxford in these years. Their father was a mountaineer too and he introduced them early to the Alpine season. 'We went up a glacier,' wrote Aldous, the youngest, in a letter, 'and father pulled me about on a rope and we had great fun.' Julian, the eldest, found himself 'thoroughly bitten by the excitement of mountaineering, the pitting of one's human self against inhuman nature', and when he went up to Balliol he played an active part in the nocturnal roof climbing: 'There was a splendid climb on the north face of Trinity clock. This started alongside the Balliol science lab, where I had to grip the coping stones to pull myself over the gables. On one occasion the stone I was pulling on started to give way; luckily I was able to throw myself forward into position, otherwise I could easily have fallen back on to *a cheval de frise* with the stone on top of me—an unpleasant idea! Then up the west wall of Trinity, with the possibility of being confronted with a don looking out of his rooms; and so on to the clock, setting its hands wrong before returning.' Trevenen went to Balliol too, to study mathematics and classics, and at Pen-y-Pass showed himself to be a gifted rock climber. Aldous, who was to become the most famous of them all, did not go to Snowdonia until shortly before the First World War, by which time a serious eye affliction had made rock climbing impossible for him.

The Huxleys were part of the formidable Oxford contingent which also included Hugh Rose Pope, Nigel Madan, Hugh Kingsmill Lunn and his brother Arnold Lunn, who founded the Oxford Mountaineering Club, edited a book of *Oxford Mountaineering Essays* and achieved fame later as the man who introduced the British to the pleasures of ski-ing.

As might be expected from Geoffrey Young's background, the Cambridge contribution was even more impressive. It included Claude Elliott who was to become Headmaster of Eton and President of the Alpine Club; Humphrey Jones, already a lecturer in Chemistry at Clare College and the youngest Fellow of the Royal Society; and C. D. Robertson, outstanding classicist and administrator, Fellow of Trinity and secretary to the Royal Commission on Electoral Systems. Duncan Grant the artist went to Pen-y-Pass from Cambridge in these years and so did Robert Graves. And so, too, did Geoffrey Keynes—later to become a distinguished surgeon—and his brilliant brother Maynard Keynes, the man who was to dominate British economic thinking for decades. Geoffrey Young had first come across Maynard at Eton, where he was an outstanding mathematician: 'In an attempt to balance his formidable combination of intellectualism and aestheticism,' Young wrote, 'I introduced him (at a later date) to the world of open air adventure and of natural beauty. In mountain climbing he became particularly interested, even for a time enthusiastic. Delicacy of constitution prevented him maintaining the practice; which I regretted, since it might have kept the balance better.' Young took Maynard climbing from Chamonix in the summer of 1905 but the attempt to counterbalance the intense intellectual life was not as successful as he supposed. In a letter to Lytton Strachey, Maynard said: 'What rot all this is about nature; I have seen the superbest views and the wildest and most desolate expanses of snow and ice; there was even danger: but not for one single moment have I been moved with anything I can call violence.'

From the mountaineering point of view, Maynard Keynes was one of Young's rare failures though they remained friends and Keynes went to Pen-y-Pass for the hill walking and the company. The great Cambridge success was a young man called George Mallory.

Mallory was the son of a Cheshire rector. He was an adventurous boy, a great tree-climber. His younger sister wrote: ' "Impossible" was a word that acted as a challenge to him. . . . He used to climb up the down-spouts of the house, and climb about on the roof with cat-like sure-footedness.' By the age of seven he was climbing on the roof of the church.

In 1900, when he was fourteen, he went to Winchester as a mathematics scholar. He was not an outstanding student—as an intellectual he was always more earnest than accomplished—but he was a natural athlete and soon caught the eye of a young teacher, R. L. G. Irving. Irving was then at the start of a distinguished career as Alpine climber and writer. Long afterwards, he remembered the schoolboy Mallory: 'He was tallish, with long limbs, supple and not over-muscled as gymnasts are apt to be. He was extraordinarily good-looking, with a gentleness about the features and a smoothness of skin that might suggest effeminacy to a stranger; it never did to a friend.'

At Winchester Irving formed the first school mountaineering club, and Mallory was a member. In August 1904 they were in the Alps, climbing Mont Blanc, Monte Rosa and the Grand Combin. On the day after the Grand Combin climb, Mallory wrote home: 'From here we had a most interesting and in parts fairly difficult rock climb up the west aréte, which we followed for about 1,800 feet. To me this was far the most interesting part of the climb, as once the rocks were ascended we were pretty sure of the peak, and I always enjoy rock climbing more than the other part.'

His mountaineering ability probably stood him in good academic stead for it seems doubtful whether he would have been awarded an Exhibition to Magdalene College, Cambridge, on the strength of his learning alone. Luckily, the master of Magdalene, A. C. Benson, was a keen Alpinist, and Mallory went up to read history in 1905. He was a good oarsman, took a serious interest in cultural and social matters and soon had a circle of friends which included Geoffrey Keynes, Hugh Wilson and Rupert Brooke.

In September 1907 he spent a vigorous week in North Wales with Wilson and Geoffrey Keynes. They stayed at Gwern-y-Gof-Isaf, bathed several times a day in streams and lakes, and climbed hard. They were, in fact, the 'three young climbers' whose clumsiness on the Terminal Aríte on Lliwedd had shaken Archer Thomson and caused him to call the new route he was making nearby the Avalanche Route.

Mallory was back in Snowdonia the next summer, this time staying at Pen-y-Pass with his young brother, Trafford. It was during this holiday that he soloed the climb which is still called Mallory's Slab and graded 'Very Difficult'. Half a century later Geoffrey Young described the incident:

> The feat was entirely in the Mallory vein; but it was not so accidental as it may sound. Many of us were concerned with that large unclimbed facet, and while lunching on the terrace above it we had been looking down and discussing it. In the evening George—only an occasional smoker—remembered leaving his pipe on the ledge. Next morning, in the first sunshine, when the rest of the Shack ran up to bathe in the ittle lake, George ran up the opposite way, on to Lliwedd, up the Slab, down by the easier way, and back in time for our traditionally late breakfast at Pen-y-Pass. On the next day a large party of us repeated the climb.

Mallory's good looks and unaffected charm created some emotional embarrassments for him. There seem to have been a remarkable number of romantically handsome young men in Edwardian England, and particularly in Edwardian Cambridge,'city of paradox and pederasty'. Lytton Strachey, an unabashed homosexual at a time when it was still dangerous to be so open about it, was the intellectual leader of the University's brighter spirits and found himself a rival sometimes with Maynard Keynes and Duncan Grant for the affections of the more attractive recruits to their elitist society, the Apostles. He met Mallory for the first time in the spring of 1909 and wrote an astonishing letter to Clive and Vanessa Bell:

> Mon Dieu!—George Mallory! When that's been written, what more need be said? My hand trembles, my heart palpitates, my whole being swoons away at the words—. . . he's six feet high, with the body of an athlete by Praxiteles, and a face—oh incredible—the mystery of Botticelli, the refinement and delicacy of a Chinese print, the

youth and piquancy of an unimaginable English boy. . . To have sat
with him in the King's garden among violets and cherry blossom, to
have—no, no for desire was lost in wonder, and there was profana-
tion even in a kiss. . . . For the rest he's going to be a schoolmaster,
and his intelligence is not remarkable. What's the need?

Although Strachey protested that his feelings for Mallory were 'more
idealistic than sensual', it was probably fortunate that this was Mallory's
last term at Cambridge and he was again immersed in the climbing
scene. He was at Pen-y-Pass that Easter and looking forward to the
Alpine season—his first for four years—with Geoffrey Young and
Donald Robertson. There was no danger that he would be pursued
there. Strachey had nothing but contempt for what he called 'imbecile
mountains'. After a visit to Skye, where he found the Sligachan Hotel
offensively full of fishermen and climbers, Geoffrey Young had challenged him about the Cuillin and said, 'Even you must admit there is
something impressive in those great dark profiles against the sea.'
Strachey replied in his famous falsetto: 'I think them . . . *simply* . . .
absurd!'

Mallory got a job as an assistant master at Charterhouse at £270 a
year. He taught mainly history and English and was given a rough
time by Philistine boys who took advantage of his serious and gentle
nature. But he was able to establish close relationships with a few of
the brighter boys—'From the first,' wrote Robert Graves, 'he treated
me as an equal'—and he introduced them to climbing at Pen-y-Pass.

Another group which went to Pen-y-Pass regularly in these years
and made a distinctive contribution was that which came from Ireland. It included Page Dickinson, Frank Sparrow the architect, and
Conor O'Brien who sailed his ketch across the Irish Sea to anchor off
Caernarvon. O'Brien was later to become famous when he sailed his
small boat round the world in 1923, ostensibly to join a mountaineering party in the New Zealand Alps. At Pen-y-Pass in the pre-War days
he was noted for his loquacity and the fact that he always climbed in
bare feet. Robert Graves recalled climbing with him and his sister, Kitty,
in the spring of 1914:

Conor climbed, he told us, principally as a corrective to bad nerves. He would get very excited when any slight hitch occurred; his voice usually rose to a scream. Kitty used to chide him: 'Ach, Conor, dear, have a bit of wit!' and Conor would apologize. Being a sailor, he used to climb in bare feet. Often in climbing one has to support the entire weight of one's body on a couple of toes—but toes in stiff boots. Conor claimed that he could force his naked toes farther into crevices than a boot would go.

The Irish brought their own special qualities of light-hearted imaginativeness to Snowdonia. Young records that once, when he complained to them about a very long and very noisy ascent of theirs, they gave a new definition of lead climbing: 'You see we *all* wanted *our* turns at leading—that is kicking and throwing stones down at the rest.' There was a proposal that the poet, W. B. Yeats, might be invited over with them but Young thought his romantic absent-mindedness might make him altogether too dangerous on the crags.

These several streams came together at Pen-y-Pass with the Snowdonia pioneers and Geoffrey Young's other friends. Charles Trevelyan, Liberal M.P. and Parliamentary Secretary to the Board of Education, was often there; so were George Trevelyan the historian and Vincent Baddeley, Financial Secretary to the Treasury. Another regular was A. D. Godley, a great classical scholar and Fellow of Magdalen, who, as Public Orator of Oxford University, had the task of making witty remarks in Latin about visiting dignitaries. Godley was a remarkable man—a keen climber in the Alps and the Lake District and North Wales, an accomplished writer of elegant light verse, but so self-effacing in company that he was often thought to be half asleep. Maynard Keynes said, 'He has the reputation of being the dullest man in Oxford to talk to, and of being the greatest wit in print.' He could be quick-witted on the crags, too. A. W. Andrews was with him on Tryfan when Godley slipped and fell about six feet into the bed of a gully, saying as he landed, 'If I had been quicker I should have said I was going to jump.'

There were occasional maverick visitors too, and none more maverick than Horace de Vere Cole, the man who had conquered the Great Gate Route in Trinity. Cole was rich and wayward, physically very courageous and much given to practical joking. It was he who master-minded the great con-trick of 1910, when he alerted the Royal Navy to expect a visit from the Emperor of Abyssinia and his retinue, and per-suaded his Bloomsbury friends—including Virginia Woolf and Duncan Grant—to black up and assume outlandish costumes. He got the party officially welcomed to the Home Fleet at Weymouth and ceremoni-ously shown round the top-secret Dreadnought, chiefly by virtue of his own masterly impersonation of a Foreign Office official and inter-preter. After the triumph he tipped off the Press and created a national furore. Making mock of the Royal Navy almost amounted in those days to high treason. There were pompous questions about it in the House of Commons. And Cole was delighted. He was an unpredictable man to climb with, as Young discovered in the Lake District:

> I doubt if Horace Cole ever played off a more dangerous practical joke than when on a day he was climbing alone with me on Scafell that winter. He was of striking appearance and physique, with heavy dark hair and immense dark-blue eyes. He was also for a time, a bold climber. We had just managed to make the first ascent of the lowest and unclimbed pitch on Collier's Climb, on Scafell, by an insidious use of the right-sized pebble under my heel on the sloping slab. Well out upon the higher cliff face and above a longish run-out, I called down to him to follow. He shouted, 'Are you quite sound?' to which I shouted in answer, 'Safe as a house!' On the in-stant, I saw his figure flash straight out from the unseen wall below me, in a headlong dive, and the next second the whole of his consid-erable weight and impetus came on to me and my belay. It was the jester's way of challenging my veracity, and—it was playing the fool in dire earnest!

The Pen-y-Pass gatherings introduced women into British rock climbing. One or two women had climbed, and climbed hard, in the Lake District, but the community at the Wastwater Hotel had been overwhelmingly masculine. At Pen-y-Pass, however, women were welcomed not only at the evening festivities but on the cliffs as well. Ursula Nettleship, the singer, was one of them, and Humphrey Jones' sister, Bronwen. There was Mrs Nettleton—according to Geoffrey Young, 'the first of women climbers to step lightly up difficult slabs'. Eleanor Slingsby, fifteen years old, was escorted by her elder brother Laurence to Pen-y-Pass at Easter 1911 and Young led them up Gashed Crag on Tryfan. And during the same holiday a party that ascended the Great Gully of Craig yr Ysfa included Mrs K. J. P. Orton, and a young friend of Mallory's called Cottie Sanders who was to become famous as the novelist Ann Bridge.

That year, 1911, probably marks the high point. Most of the regulars and some newcomers were there at Easter and there was much high-spirited fun and a lot of climbing. Eckenstein brought along his Austrian guide, Dr Karl Blodig, who amused Young by saying the two things a man needed in the mountains were 'butter and alcohol' and who entertained the company by singing 'The Watch on the Rhine'. Young's Alpine season that summer was impressive even by his standards, including first ascents of the Brouillard Ridge of Mont Blanc from the Col Emile Rey, the West Ridge of the Grandes Jorasses and the Mer de Glace face of the Grepon. And he was at Pen-y-Pass again for 'the most glorious of all parties' that Christmas. Mallory was there too and a new contingent from Oxford. It was after this gathering that Young wrote the sadly prophetic note in his diary: 'We all knew such a time could hardly repeat.'

As all such close-knit communities do, they created around them a web of traditions and jokes. They enjoyed the idiosyncracies of their companions. They liked to start the day gently: 'We used to take a leisurely breakfast,' Robert Graves remembered, 'and lie in the sun with a tankard of beer before starting for the precipice foot in the late morning.' Once on the move, though, they climbed hard and usually found time for a bathe on the way home. It was traditional to spend Easter Day and Christmas Day on Tryfan (Plate 22), climbers and walkers joining together for the walk there and back, and the final half-day of the holiday on Dinas Mot, usually in the Black Cleft.

Some of their jokes had a strong literary flavour. On one occasion C. K. Clague, a devotee of the works of Lewis Carroll, fell some fifty feet on Lliwedd. He was held on the rope, and was heard soon after

22. *The East face of Tryfan, perennially popular with rock climbers.
(Photograph by Carl Rogers.)*

quoting the Red King: 'I advise you fellows to come down the regular way and not by the volcano!' Page Dickinson is said to have been seen hurling a piece of rock that had come away in his hands to the scree below with a cry of 'Lie there, lie there, false strata!' Perhaps most memorable of all was Claude Elliott's reported advice to Ursula Nettleship at a tricky moment during her first encounter with the Teryn Slab: 'Better not put more than one foot on the same hold as your two hands.'

Geoffrey Young liked to give a literary touch to the naming of new routes. After Archer Thomson had named one of his East Buttress routes on Lliwedd the Red Wall, Young called his alternative the Purple Passage because 'it was that kind of passage and better left out'. And he named the Solomon Climb because it concluded by exactly bisecting a feature that was known as the Quartz Babe. One famous place name on Lliwedd, the 'Thank God hold' on Route 2, has a disputed derivation. Young says that he christened it after a party of Irishmen he was leading had each successively used the same expression of gratitude when his hands found the big hold. But A. W. Andrews claims he bestowed the name when Percy Farrar reached the same place and 'expressed his feelings with some frankness . . . I had never seen the phrase in literature before my description, but it has evidently taken the popular fancy as everyone claims the first use of it.'

In the years leading up to the First World War the parties included many whose achievements earned them a permanent place in the history of climbing. One of them was Leslie Shadbolt, a great pioneer on Skye and a member of the first party to make the traverse of the Cuillin ridge in a single expedition. Another, George Ingle Finch, was to climb with Mallory on Everest in the 1920s. From the purely rock-climbing point of view, the most important was a young engineering student from Manchester University called Siegfried Wedgwood Herford. Although he was born in Aberystwyth and had visited the Alps in his mid-teens, it was not until he went to Manchester that he became seriously interested in climbing. There he met John Laycock and was introduced to gritstone climbing in the Pennines. Very soon he was leading climbs and inventing girdle traverses. He quickly graduated to limestone routes in Dovedale, then the bigger cliffs of Skye, the Lake District, the Dolomites and North Wales. He was reserved and gentle by nature, but outstandingly bold and skilful on the crags. In the few short years before the War he did more than any other man, perhaps, to carry rock climbing to a new standard of difficulty.

Herford's greatest achievements took place on Scafell Crag in the Lake District, in the company of G. S. Sansom. In April 1912 they solved a problem that had baffled the best of the Lakeland school for many years by finding a direct route up to Hopkinson's Cairn on the face of Scafell Pinnacle. Herford led in stockinged feet, running out the rope for a sensational 130 feet on what is now called Herford's Slab, without the benefit of any of the contrivances that protect modern leaders on such delicate and exposed ground. Two years later the same pair finally overcame, after careful reconnaissance, the challenging Central Buttress which is still graded 'Very Severe (Hard)' and was long considered the most difficult climb in the country.

Although he made no routes of comparably sustained severity in Wales, Herford climbed well enough around Pen-y-Pass to be elected to Geoffrey Young's special trinity:

As all-round mountaineers, three men, as dissimilar in their physical perfection as in their powers of mind, stand out in recollection among their gifted contemporaries: Hugh Rose Pope, Siegfried W. Herford, and George Leigh Mallory. It is unlikely that any mountaineering generation will see again the association of three more outstanding personalities. Pope, prodigious in his height, reach, splendid physique and controlled method, the product of cultivated atmospheres, with a typically Etonian and leisurely manner, a large, dark, humorous eye for all human ways, and, underneath, the soul of romance and poetic adventure. Herford, shapely, powerful, with a wind-blown fair mane and blue thoughtful eyes, scientific in his interests, a poet at heart, coming and going at our meetings with the spontaneousness of the wind, so near to the light and wonder of the hills in spirit that his feats upon their cliffs seemed only natural. Mallory, the last to survive, was the greatest in his fulfilled achievement, and possibly the first man to reach the summit of the world's surface; so original in his climbing that it never occurred to us to compare him with others or judge his performance by ordinary mountaineering standards. A Galahad (as he was called): chivalrous, indomitable, the splendid personification of youthful adventure; deer-like in grace and power of movement, self-reliant and yet self-effacing, and radiantly independent. On a day he might be with us; on the next gone like a bird on the wing over the summits, to explore some precipice between Snowdon and the sea; whence he would return after nightfall to discuss climbs or metaphysics in a laughing contralto, or practise gymnastics after his hot bath, on the roof-beam of the old shack, like the youngest of the company.

They were a privileged and varied and talented group of people and in those few years, between 1907 and 1914, they formed a unique and very happy community. Many years later, Cottie Sanders recalled one evening in the hotel during the Easter holiday of 1911 when George Mallory and one of the Irishmen fell into a long argument about whether a man should have principles or not:

I have a picture of the group now: Mrs. Reade on one side of the fire; the Irishman opposite, with his feet over the arm of his chair, mowing down opposed theories with the skill of a good fencer; George on the floor between them, his hands round his knees, unclasped now and then to throw back his hair, stammering a little with his eagerness and impatience and the difficulty of getting out what he had to say, but getting it out all the same; while in corners pairs expounded their views to one another or put in a quick word, and a big black-haired Munsterman drummed with his fists on the bookcase and talked about Bentham.

Chapter X

NEW ROUTES, 1906-14

... those moments when, with heart of youth,
forgetful of the fetters of our mind,
we battle with the might
of some vast precipice . . .

THEY kept a book at Pen-y-Pass on the model of the Locked Book at Pen-y-Gwryd. It has survived the transformation of the hotel into a youth hostel and the dispersal of the Climbers' Club library. A sturdy, folio-sized, leather-bound volume, its front cover is inscribed with the words 'For Climbing and Scientific Notes Only'. In fact, it contains no scientific notes but plenty of terse, factual accounts of new climbs accomplished and comments, sometimes helpful, sometimes critical. It is a useful source of information, particularly for the years 1906 to 1914 when the cliffs of Snowdonia were alive with activity.

New routes abound; new cliffs were discovered; and new names appear, not all of them connected with Geoffrey Young's circle.

For a week in August 1906, for example, a party of four men who make no other appearance in this story, concentrated their attention on Cyrn Las. Their names were A. E. Barker, H. Mitchell, W. J. Drew and G. T. Atchison. On the 6th, Barker led them up Yellowstone Gully at the western end of the crag. Three days later Mitchell found a way up the gully just to the left which they called Double Cave Gully. And on the 12th, Mitchell led them up a more exacting 300-foot route which they called the Schoolmasters' Gully 'for while parsons, doctors, engineers and professors have their special climbs, none has so far been dedicated to the profession to which three of our party belong.' The route is still graded 'Hard Very Difficult', and Atchison's description of their climb includes a passage which will raise echoes in the minds of many climbers:

From this grass platform, which we termed the 'Bowling Green', we traversed to the left round a projecting rock back into the centre of the gully, and then worked up the left face to another sloping grass platform, to which we gave the name the 'Croquet Ground'. This traverse round the projecting rock was the source of considerable amusement. Each of us insisted that the man before him made a ridiculous fuss, and spent an absurdly long time over it. Criticism and advice flowed freely, but each of us modified his opinion when his own turn came. Our difficulty arose from a desire to find a more substantial hold for the left hand than that provided by Faith and Hope. We failed to find one.

The year before this, Walter Parry Haskett Smith had made his own individual contribution to Snowdonian climbing by discovering the possibilities of the crags above Llyn Cwellyn, south-west of the Snowdon massif. He liked the region for its quiet—these crags were untouched by climbing boots until he came—and for its accessibility. A dilapidated little railway, the North Wales Narrow Gauge, took passengers from the main coastal line at Dinas Junction up to the lake and beyond. In the course of an active foray with Geoffrey Hastings into this area in 1905 he climbed Wolf's Buttress on Castell Cidwm, the Pinnacle Ridge and other routes on Craig y Bera, and the Eastern Arête on Y Garn, a 430-foot climb which is still graded 'Very Difficult' and is one of the most popular routes in the area.

Although Haskett Smith made his discovery promptly known in the pages of *The Climbers' Club Journal*, six more years passed before Archer Thomson and H. O. Jones launched an intensive assault on these crags to be quickly followed by the formidable rope of Mallory and H. E. L. Porter. Several routes that are still graded 'Severe' were then made and one is graded 'Very Severe', Mallory's Ridge on Y Garn. According to the current Climbers' Club guide-book this route was not repeated until September 1949.

Throughout the period the main interest continued to centre on Lliwedd. Its height and breadth and intricacy made the possibilities seem inexhaustible. By 1914 the great cliff was studded with more than forty routes that were identified and named, and many others so rambling and convoluted that they defied subsequent recognition. Archer Thomson was still the great authority, with Andrews not far behind. Among the newer men the names that recur most often are Humphrey Jones, George Mallory and Geoffrey Young.

The three years, 1907-1910, saw enormous activity here—a total of seventeen new routes, which include Archer Thomson's Girdle Traverse and Avalanche Route, Mallory's Slab and Wrong Chimney, and Humphrey Jones' Slanting Gully Rib and Paradise Climb.

Thomson and Andrews' guide-book *The Climbs on Lliwedd* was published in the summer of 1909 and Humphrey Jones and R. F. Blackwell were armed with a copy when they set off from Pen-y-Pass one morning in September that year to see if there was any part of the Heather Shelf area still open to exploration. They published an account of the resulting climb in *The Climbers' Club Journal*:

Near the east end of the Heather Shelf a number of ribs and cracks mount at a very steep angle to a distinct grass ledge, about seventy feet above, near the east end of which there are two small mountain ash trees, one above the other: this grass ledge was the first objective. One of the ribs was first ascended for a few feet, then with the aid of a good hold for the hands on another rib to the left a bold stride was made over this intervening rib into a waterworn groove or crack. This crack and a chimney above were ascended to a sound grass stance only a few feet below the aforementioned grass ledge. The ascent was effected chiefly by means of small rounded (waterworn) holds, which naturally all sloped the wrong way; the climbing was difficult, and the strain severe until one's body was raised on to the grass stance from which the grass ledge was easily reached. At the east end of this ledge there is standing room for one and there are two belays. One of these, about six feet above the ledge, can be used to give security to the second man while the leader can utilise the rope jammed in a crack and placed over the other belay. When the second had ascended to this point a few steps were taken along the ledge to the west, round an awkward corner, and the ascent continued by means of a quartz vein which proved to be more difficult than expected; this soon landed the party on a second grass ledge. This ledge sloped downwards and to the east to an extent that rendered it unsuitable for a prolonged rest . . . A steep slab on the left, facing north west, looked attractive, the holds were small but square cut and sloped the right way, and about forty feet of excellent climbing led to a stance from which a small grass shelf, dominated by a deeply cut sloping recess with an overhanging roof, could be seen on the right. This grass shelf was soon reached by ascending easy rocks and traversing a few feet to the right, and it proved to be a welcome haven. It was approximately flat, and would seat three comfortably, so a much needed rest was taken there, and proved so delightful to the weary climbers that it was decided forthwith to call this luxurious resting place 'Paradise,' and to give the same name to the route when completed. Later on a thick streak of quartz on the right was diligently quarried, and 'Paradise' was adorned with a cairn of noble dimensions, which notably diminishes the seating accommodation.

At Easter that year W. R. Reade and Geoffrey Bartrum made the first route up the steep back of Central Gully. The problem had defeated many previous parties. Named Reade's Crack, it is the only route on Lliwedd made before the First World War which is still graded 'Severe'.

Geoffrey Young's achievement was continuing and considerable. In 1907 he led the Roof Route, in 1912 Purple Passage, and in 1914, alternating the lead with H. E. L. Porter, he bisected the Quartz Babe with Solomon. But his most impressive contribution, perhaps, was the double girdle of the whole breadth of the cliff, from east to west, then back again at a higher level. His companions were Mallory and Herford and their swift, arduous accomplishment must have owed much to their Alpine training in sustained effort *(Plate 23)*. In *Mountains with a Difference* Young described the day rhapsodically:

. . . . as some people remember music, I now recall my view either way across the Lliwedd precipices storming up the sky under ghostly downfalls of ice, forward and back to the agile figures in white sweaters, swinging, turning, belaying in a counterpoint of precision and force, as the occasional sun-gleam glinted from one or other of the rough fair heads white-rimmed with frost from the shadows. Alike in so much and in their generous emulation, the difference in climbing styles was striking: Mallory, undulating upward or along the crags; Herford, upright, in quick steel-smooth balances. We serpentined over the snowy buttresses, seeking out the best passages. At the end, we threw in the Slanting slab, and then turned up the outside Needle ridge, to lunch on a shelf The white edges of the lake far below looked crisp with wind-rippled ice, and far above on the left the enormous snow-cone of Y Wyddfa was ringed with wisps of snow-cloud, in a wind we did not feel. It was all too good to leave. Why make an end? We dropped down a ridge to a promising level, and then re-crossed the whole face once more, on a higher and even more exacting line over bastion, wall and chasm. It was the first double Girdle. We travelled on the return even faster, and in a rhythm which I never remember attaining again on stiff rock with a rope of three.

There were further advances, too, on the cliffs around Cwm Glas. Geoffrey Young and Conor O'Brien made a girdle traverse of Clogwyn y Ddysgl; and with another partner, Harold Porter, Young discovered the climb that is still named after him on Clogwyn Pen Llechen. But the best contribution came from the formidable rope of W. R. Reade and Geoffrey Bartrum, Reade's Route on Crib Goch Buttress.

On the cliffs to the north of Pen-y-Pass much of the new work was being done by groups which had little or no connection with the Pen-y-Pass circle—by Dr Guy Barlow of Birmingham University and his most constant companion, E. W. Steeple, and by the Abraham brothers and their Lakeland friends.

'We had been a merry party of four at Gwern-y-Gof-Isaf during the latter days of October 1904.' The tone of voice is unmistakable. The Abraham brothers were back in North Wales to extend their conquests

23. Siegfried Herford (left) and George Mallory, resting against the wall of the Pen-y-Pass hotel after their double girdle of Lliwedd with Geoffrey Young. (Photograph by Geoffrey Young.)

and gather material for their projected book which was to do for Snowdonia what O. G. Jones' classic had done for the Lake district. Their companions were C. W. Nettleton and A. W. Wakefield, a record-breaking fell walker, and they introduced them to the Milestone Buttress *(Plate 24)* and recorded two new routes further afield, the Ridge Route on Lliwedd and Vanishing Gully on Craig yr Ysfa.

They were back at the little farmhouse the following Easter. It rained continuously for six days. 'My experience of Welsh farmhouses,' George wrote, 'has not been altogether a pleasant one. Somehow these domiciles have become associated in my mind with small windows, blinding rain, and inexhaustible mutton.' They had better luck a few weeks later when they returned for a more fruitful visit with J. W. Puttrell and two climbers from Kendal, Darwen Leighton and Andrew Thomson. They made three excellent new routes, Amphitheatre Buttress on Craig

24. On the Milestone Buttress, 1904. George Abraham watches, A. W. Wakefield stretches. (Photograph by the Abraham brothers.)

yr Ysfa, Monolith Crack on the Gribin Facet and Hawk's Nest Buttress on Glyder Fach.

Hawk's Nest Buttress was the Abrahams' finest achievement in North Wales, comparable with their other great routes, the New West on Pillar Rock in the Lake District and Crowberry Ridge on Buachaille Etive Mor in Glencoe. It is 185 feet long and still graded 'Severe'. Colin Kirkus described it as 'A very fine climb, clean and steep and exposed.

148

Much of the climbing is strenuous and there is at least one movement of great delicacy in an airy situation.'

As usual George led, supported by his brother Ashley and Andrew Thomson, and his account of the crux middle pitches lost nothing in his telling:

> ... the rock was magnificent, and afforded no more than just sufficient hold for the safe ascent. The first stretch of about twenty feet proved to be rather a study in finger-tip holds; but some assistance was derived from gripping the rough edges of a narrow vertical rock-rib with the knees.
>
> A small ledge now afforded a resting-place, so my brother was able to come up to steady my feet on the tiny holds that just rendered the next section possible. Though only fifteen feet high, it proved to be the crux of the climb; and the situation was quite exposed enough to make our companion's call of warning unnecessary. The difficulty of the place was aggravated by the annoying antics of the hawks. Their nest was only a few yards round a corner on our left, and they kept swooping down above my head. A well-aimed piece of Glyder from our sheet-anchor rather allayed their aggressiveness, and I was able at last to reach a comforting hand-hold at the top of this engrossing section.

During the same holiday they made one other intriguing expedition, to Clogwyn du'r Arddu. They prospected about hopefully, wondered at the blank steepness of the great walls— 'The sensation of height sent a thrill through one's whole anatomy,' wrote Ashley—and finally made their way up a little route above the Eastern Terrace which they called the East Wall Climb. It was not an important ascent and it is rarely visited nowadays, but it was the first new route on 'Cloggy' for more than a century and Ashley's reflective paragraph about it in the brothers' book may have done something to revive interest in the crag:

> It would be a rash thing to say that the cracks straight up the north face of the Clogwyn will never be ascended. Climbs are accomplished nowadays that would have been deemed incredible forty years ago, and it will be interesting to see what the next generation does on the

rocks which at present, by general consent, are considered too steep and dangerous. Should that future generation produce men far in advance of the present rock-climbers in the art of scaling steep places, they will find many first ascents awaiting them on Clogwyn Du'r-arddu.

Other parties were now at work on the cliffs above Ogwen. On Milestone Buttress, Guy Barlow led his sister on first ascents on the Direct Route and Pulpit Route and Ivy Chimney. On the Gribin Facet, O. Thorneycroft found a short but strenuous climb on the Flake Crack. In 1912 Herford and Laycock brought their training on gritstone to bear on Welsh granite with three new climbs on the Gribin Facet and two 'Severes', Square Chimney and Alpha, on the main cliff of Glyder Fach. Guy Barlow and Mrs Daniell, who was to be the first woman to lead a new route, created the Central Arête Direct on the Upper Cliff of Glyder Fawr.

On Tryfan, strangely, there was a long hiatus after the discovery of the Gashed Crag route in 1902. Eight years later Barlow and E. W. Steeple prospected a possible new line on the North Buttress but did not get very far. They returned a year later—at Easter 1911—to make a more determined assault with three friends, A. G. Woodhead, H. E. Bowron, and A. H. Doughty. The result was a 700-foot climb that has been a great favourite ever since, Grooved Arête, which is given the honour of a three-star grading in Ron James' guide to the best routes in Snowdonia. Steeple's account of the first ascent in *The Climbers' Club Journal* modestly omitted to name the leader:

A breezy ascent for some 75 feet on splendidly sound rock led to an overhang, where a divergence from the strict arête was found necessary. A step was therefore taken to the left into the long central groove previously mentioned. This was ascended with some difficulty for 10 feet to a ledge about 1½ inches wide, on the right wall. The second man now climbed into the groove, and belayed his rope by means of a deep cleft behind the little ledge. The groove is closed in above by a continuation of the overhang, and a difficult stride was made round a corner on the left, marked by a diminutive ash-tree. A cautious pull up a thin edge of rock then brought the leader to a heather shelf (the Haven), furnished with a good belay-pin. The whole party assembled here.

This point had been reached by Dr. Barlow and myself in 1910, but we were then unable to make any impression on the upper part of the groove, which, owing to a curious contortion of the strata, overhangs the lower part. On this second occasion Barlow gave me a shoulder, but I was stopped a few feet higher by a bulge of rock in the groove. Woodhead then made an attempt, but with no better success, and we finally decided that the pitch was unjustifiable. Moreover, the large slab on the left of the groove gives a much finer route. (Barlow had suggested this possibility on our first visit, but I then thought the place looked rather hopeless.)

Near the south end of the Haven a few feet of moderately easy rock and a short grassy cleft gave access to the commencement of this slab. I did not like the look of the place any better on a second inspection, and the credit of the successful issue is due to Woodhead, who came up with a little pick, and with infinite patience cleared out a line of small holds up the slab. These run at first to the right, then straight up to a small rock recess, about 50 feet above the Haven. A boss of loose rock on the left should be avoided.

From the recess a traverse was made to the right across a bulging mass at the top of the slab to a little platform in the groove, above the troublesome part. An exit from this delightful nook was made on to the edge of the true arête on the right, which was followed until a narrow ledge was seen sloping upwards along the vertical wall of the Green Gully. This ledge is rather sensational, but good hand-holds were found where they were most needed, and from the farther end a large grass platform was easily reached. An alternative route to this platform can be made by stepping back into the groove above the steep wall behind the 'nook', and climbing two little pitches. The variation is not so interesting, however, as the traverse of the ledge.

The remaining 100 feet of rock are remarkably steep, but furnished with excellent holds, and we arrived at the shoulder, or 'Low Man' of the Buttress, a few yards to the north of the cairn marking the ordinary route.

A distinctive finish was given to the climb by the ascent of a series of cracks and two sharp-pointed pinnacles immediately in front of us on the North Peak. This route commences some distance to the north of the 'wing of rock' generally used, and at a lower level.

The climb here described is longer than the other buttress climbs on the East Face, and, with the exception of the neighbouring Terrace Wall Variant, more difficult, and should only be attempted by an experienced party. It is, however, a climb of considerable variety and much interest. A party of three would probably be the best number, and 60 feet of rope will be found sufficient between each man.

Grooved Arête is today graded 'Hard Very Difficult'. The following year Steeple and Barlow created the Chimney Route on Milestone Buttress which is still graded 'Severe'.

Throughout all this time the old school was far from idle. Archer Thomson continued to investigate Lliwedd, gave attention to the remoter cliffs beyond Llyn Cwellyn, and in 1910 discovered a new cliff which he claimed was 'the most important addition to the climber's domain since the annexation of Craig yr Ysfa in 1900'. The discovery was cunningly used by the Climbers' Club to whip up interest in Thomson's forthcoming guide-book *Climbing in the Ogwen District*, but when the secret was revealed the new cliff turned out to be Creigiau Gleision which others failed to find so exciting. Thomson, however, explored it vigorously and was able to list six routes in the guide-book. His description of the Tower Ridge is a typical example of Thomson's style:

About eighty feet higher the climber is confronted by an overhanging proboscis. On its left side is a green ledge, which gives access to a short, vertical chimney. The closed fist fitted in prevents the body falling out. By this fissure the edge of the ridge is regained. A short distance above the leader can sit in comfort astride of it, and bitt the rope round a stook of bollards. On the arrival of the next man he climbs up a thin edge for fifteen feet to a second saddle-seat, with a pommel of rock in front. The final portion is a very steep slab of repellent aspect. Its centre is seamed by a shallow groove of twenty-five feet. This furnishes small but adequate holds, which it may be necessary to unearth with a penknife. The ascent is perhaps more impressive than really difficult, but strict attention to balance is essential. The slab leads up to the top of the Tower (cairn).

This climb gratifies the taste for romantic situations.

His best route on Creigiau Gleision was the Great Ridge which he described as:

Exceedingly difficult. Delectable in good weather; inadvisable in bad. Interest well sustained throughout. Only for a thoroughly expert party. Leader requires sixty feet of rope, and cannot be aided on the hardest passages. . . . The climbing, continuous throughout, is of a high order; neither is the climber anywhere compelled to the handling of soil or plants.

In 1911 four undergraduates made another route on Creigiau Gleision, the Central Ridge. They were Hugh Rose Pope, Nigel Madan, Claude Elliott and Trevenen Huxley. They had been close friends since their days at Eton, when Geoffrey Young was a teacher there. In 1909 they holidayed together at Wasdale and, inspired by the books of O. G. Jones and the Abrahams, began rock climbing. From the first, Pope was their leader, tall and strong, with natural balance and an equable temperament. The next year they were enlisted into the Pen-y-Pass parties. In 1911 they were back in the Lake District to attempt the formidable Walker's Gully on Pillar Rock. Pope was in the lead but finally admitted himself defeated, just below the crux, by the atrocious weather and the great volume of water pouring down the gully. On the way down, when Elliott was abseiling off, a falling rock severed the rope and he fell, seriously damaging a knee.

More than sixty years later, at his home at the head of Buttermere, Sir Claude Elliott—as he had by then become—said this accident had almost certainly saved his life. It kept him out of climbing for several years and rendered him unfit for a combatant role in the War. Within five years all his friends were dead. Pope died in a mountaineering accident; Huxley committed suicide; Nigel Madan was killed at Ypres.

Chapter XI

CLOTHING, EQUIPMENT & TECHNIQUES

With each strong thrust
I feel all motion and all vital force
borne on my strength and hazarding their course
in my self-trust.

THE modern rock climber is an unmistakable sight. His protective clothing, wind-proofs and water-proofs and crash helmet, are picked out in strong, bright colours. On his feet, for maximum adhesion to small holds, he wears rubber-soled boots. Over one shoulder he carries slings of rope or tape, each one bearing a metal karabiner. He wears a webbing harness round his waist, and there are more karabiners clipped to this and attached to a further armoury of loops and metal nuts of various sizes. If the route is particularly serious, he will also carry a range of metal pegs, pitons, and a hammer and possibly a couple of étriers or short rope ladders. The climbing rope—or ropes—running from his waist will be made of nylon and usually 150 feet long. And all this equipment has been specially designed and manufactured to combine the greatest possible strength and reliability with the least possible weight.

The men who climbed before 1914 had none of these aids. The only things that distinguished them from hill walkers were their heavily nailed boots and what they called their 'Alpine ropes'. Their clothing was thick and heavy, exactly the same as would be worn by any countryman in uncertain weather. This was George Abraham's advice in his book *The Complete Mountaineer*: ' . . . the climber's apparel throughout should be entirely of wool, though it may be found necessary for the sake of a stronger texture to procure coat and knickerbockers containing a small proportion of cotton. The Norfolk jacket is undoubtedly the best form of coat, and it should contain at least six pockets made by preference of strong flannel. . . . A warm waistcoat is a great comfort, and the most important feature of it should be a thick flannel lining down the back.' And Geoffrey Young recalled: 'In the beginning we all used to wear much heavier climbing garments, both upper and under; and the weight of corduroys and wools and leathers and armoured boots when they were all wet through, much encumbered pioneer ascents.' *(Plate 25)*. The crash helmet was already being used by motor-cyclists but it would be many years before climbers accepted its advantages.

The vital article of clothing was the boots. Conor O'Brien climbed bare-footed and A. W. Andrews in tennis shoes, but the great majority of the early climbers wore sturdy leather boots with a variety of nails hammered into the soles and heels in a variety of patterns. 'I have no hesitation,' George Abraham wrote, 'in saying that a pair of properly nailed boots are, or should be, the most important details of a climber's outfit . . . the leathers for the uppers should be the best zug or chrome, soft and absolutely waterproof. The heels should be low, and they, as well as the soles, should project fully a quarter of an inch beyond the uppers when new. . . . The nailing of climbing boots is a fine art. The greatest skill is required in driving the nails direct, for it is imperative that no hole should be previously bored in the leather, otherwise they will come out sooner or later, generally sooner.' The precise arrangement of the nails was the subject of much discussion. George Abraham recommended an outside ring of large wrought-iron nails, overlapping each other, all round the soles and heels, with a pattern of smaller nails inside. But Percy Farrar thought overlapping edge nails were absurd and Geoffrey Young said, 'the chief thing for rock is to make sure that the edge nails, whatever they be, are set well apart, so as to give a rough catching edge between each nail against a pull either

BURBERRY Outfits.

To withstand the severe strain of climbing, and to make provision for rapid changes of temperature, Mountaineers require garments constructed of especially manufactured textures.

BURBERRYS weatherproof materials, woven and proofed by Burberry processes, are just what the Mountaineer requires and when made into outfits under expert advice, the climber enjoys to the full his hazardous pursuit, with an assurance of all the comfort possible.

BURBERRY
MOUNTAINEERING GOWN.

The BURBERRY outfit displays the utmost economy in weight, with phenomenal durability.

Proof against rain, sleet, wind and cold, yet retains perfect self-ventilation. Practical in form and perfected by inventions that preserve absolute limb freedom.

Full particulars and patterns of the materials that experience has shown to give the best results, write for
BURBERRY-PROOF CLIMBING KIT.
Post free on application.

BURBERRY
MOUNTAINEERING
OUTFIT.

BURBERRYS,
30 to 33, Haymarket, LONDON.
PARIS: 10, Boul. Malesherbes.

25. *An advertisement from 'The Climbers' Club Journal' of 1909.*

way. . . . One good rough nail rightly driven in and rightly placed is quite enough to ensure a perfectly safe stance under a well-balanced body; and on much modern slab climbing one nail-hold is all that is sought or obtained. The neater the action the fewer the nails needed.'

In the matter of clothing, the women pioneers were much more handicapped than the men. Right up to 1914, propriety required that their legs should be voluminously concealed beneath long skirts. They must have felt uncomfortable and clumsy at all times and particularly in hot weather, and found it impossible to see exactly where they were putting their feet. But their aunts and mothers had climbed in the Alps in full-length skirts for decades, and it took a great deal of courage to defy the conventions. Twenty years later one of the best of the pioneer women climbers, Mrs Daniell, remembered the problems: 'A woman in knickerbockers was an object of derision or shame. Even as late as 1913 I was waylaid on the slopes of Cader Idris by what I feared was an indignantly modest female but, to my surprise, this enlightened creature wanted to congratulate me on my good sense in having discarded a skirt. The skirt was decently worn for as long as possible, then hidden under a rock or carried in a neat bundle, as circumstances decreed. Just before the war, people on the road near Ogwen would walk backwards for quite a long way, in astonishment and mirth at the sight of my sister and me in our corduroy breeches.'

The climbing rope was made of three strands of manilla hemp. It was one and a quarter inches in circumference and available in lengths of forty, sixty, eighty or a hundred feet. There seems to have been only one reputable supplier, Arthur Beale of Shaftesbury Avenue in London who had taken over the business from John Buckingham. He advertised his 'Alpine Club rope which is almost exclusively employed by the leading Mountaineers of the time' and warned readers to 'beware of fraudulent imitations'. Beale's ropes were distinguished by a length of red worsted threaded through the centre, and when an interloper used the same mark of identification Beale changed to using three red threads, one in the middle of each manilla strand. The rope was said to have been tested to withstand the strain of a twelve-stone man falling ten feet clear.

The hemp rope kinked easily and could be awkward particularly in wet conditions, but the main point of difference between early climbing and that of today lay not in the rope itself but in the way it was used.

Nowadays, the basic rules are simple and almost universally obeyed. On difficult or dangerous ground, one man climbs at a time; while he moves, his companion is concerned exclusively with managing the rope, paying it out or hauling it in as the climber advances, keeping it reasonably taut between them; and the stationary man is firmly established in position and attached, by a separate line, to the rock face behind him so that he cannot be pulled off even if the climber falls. This is what is meant by 'belaying' and over the years the technique has saved many lives. The pioneer climbers, however, meant something quite different by 'belaying' and their written accounts and photographs make it clear that they rarely used the technique properly.

They climbed simultaneously much more often than people do today, presumably because that was the general practice in the Alps where the length of the routes made it important to maintain as much speed as was reasonably possible. And even when the difficulty of the terrain forced them to climb singly, the stationary man did not, as a rule, anchor himself to the rock with a separate rope. He regarded himself, and his climbing companion, as adequately belayed if the rope between them was passed around some convenient notch or flake where it might, or might not, be expected to hold if the climber fell. And he did not, as modern climbers do, pass the rope round his back or shoulder to increase the braking friction but simply controlled it through his hands. Here is Archer Thomson, for example, on part of the Great Ridge of Creigiau Gleision: 'The situation is shelterless, but the leader, by passing his rope over a perfect belay, can protect his initial advance up the slabs. Later the rope slips off, and for this reason it would probably prove advantageous for the second man to be brought up to manipulate it.' And in the glossary to *The Climbs on Lliwedd* he defines 'belay' as 'any projection of rock round which the rope can be hitched and held'.

It is amazing how often these primitive methods seem to have proved effective. A few months before his death Sir Claude Elliott remembered: 'I usually climbed in a party of four, with a sixty-foot length of rope between each pair. We would move all together on the easier bits, but when we came to harder pitches and had to climb one at a time the stationary man didn't tie himself to anything. He just passed the rope round a notch if he could and that was standard practice in those days. He didn't work the rope round his shoulder or buttocks either, just held it in his hands. Even so, I have several times seen a leader fall and be safely held by his second.'

It did not always work, though. Several of the accidents in North Wales were directly attributable to bad rope management and so was the tragedy on Scafell in 1903 when four young men were killed. It was the worst accident in British climbing before 1954. One man slipped and his three companions, none of them anchored to the rock, were pulled off with him. The moral should have been clear: on a climb as exposed and delicate as this—they were on Herford's Slab high up on the face of Scafell Pinnacle—the way the rope was employed increased rather than diminished the danger to the whole party. It was a case of 'one off, all off'.

A few men recognized the fact and advocated the correct solution. At a northern dinner of the Climbers' Club in 1906, Cecil Slingsby said: 'In the belaying of a rope, a climber frequently interposes the hitch between the man to be belayed and himself. There should be a clear rope, as a rule, between these two; the belay being for the purpose of holding the "fixed" man if the strain should come upon him, whilst he himself should act as a kind of buffer between the moving man and the belay, in case of a slip.' Claude Benson, in his book *British Mountaineering* which was published in 1909, laid down that'... the correct procedure is for the leader to belay *himself* to the rock, so as to leave a clear rope between himself and the man following.' But Benson went on to say, 'I have stopped to insist on this method, not only because it is the best, but because, so far as I know, it is so seldom practiced that I cannot help thinking it is not generally known.',

Some climbing parties before 1914, then, knew and used the modern method, but the great majority—on most of their climbs at any rate—did not. They preferred the old, ad hoc, hopeful techniques. And though the modern method seems to have become widely accepted during the First World War, there were still climbers who rejected it. Long afterwards, for example, G. S. Sansom defended the system of passing the rope round some convenient notch on the grounds that it had served him well on several occasions and that the second man was less likely to be injured by falling rocks if he was tucked in hard against the crag instead of standing on an exposed stance with the security of a separate rope belay. And George Abraham, writing about the Scafell accident twenty years later, could conclude: 'For a height of at least 200 feet the face of the Pinnacle is one long, steep, smooth slab without any suitable projection around which the rope could be wound to secure the comparative safety of the party. Such places are seldom met with, and if they are I am quite sure that the party to attempt them should not consist of more than two experts ; in which case it is doubtful whether a rope is necessary.'

The slowness of the pioneers to adopt the sensible rope technique is all the more remarkable when one considers their ingenuity and caution in so many other ways. They used the knots which are still employed today and were insistent on the importance of tying them with the lay of the rope. They were great practitioners of 'combined operations', using each other's shoulders and heads as surrogate footholds. They devised elaborate slings and cradles of rope so that the second could help the leader in particularly difficult places. They were expert at 'threading the rope', passing it firmly behind blocked stones in cracks and chimneys to afford the leader a running belay—a technique that saved the life of O. G. Jones on more than one occasion. Some of them—the Abraham brothers in the Devil's Kitchen, for example, and Herford and Sansom on Scafell's Central Buttress—were prepared to spend a long time reconnoitering a route, sometimes with the protection of a top-rope from above, before attempting a first ascent. When they made new routes, they were careful to clean them up for the successors. It was the job of the last man on the rope to clear away all the loose rocks and vegetation.

Equipment and techniques are important factors in climbing. Ingenious methods of protecting the leader on a long run-out of rope, by the fixing of nuts and slings to afford a running belay, did a great deal to promote the rapid extension of the sport into new fields of extreme difficulty after the Second World War. But the ultimate factor is the man himself, the calibre of the climber, his skill and strength and suppleness, his experience and his capacity for calm, above all his confidence. In this respect, the pioneer rock climbers were as impressive—for their times—as the 'tigers' of later generations. They were not able to climb as frequently as their successors. They had, on the whole, scanty information about what had already been achieved on the crags they were exploring. Their methods and their gear were rudimentary by later standards, and the cliffs themselves were in a more dangerous condition, littered with the debris of ages. There was no mountain rescue organization, with vans and walkie-talkies and helicopters, to rush to their aid if things went wrong. They were explorers in the basic sense; there was no established body of information, about the theory of climbing and what had been done before them, to nourish their confidence. Their spirit was less acrimoniously competitive than that of some, at least, of their successors, and they would never have dreamed of boasting, as a few modern climbers do, of the number of times they had fallen off.

They climbed boldly but, for the most part, with cautious common sense. The golden rule was that the best climber of the party should lead and that he should not fall. George Abraham summed it up, rather severely: 'The leader must never slip. He should be incontestably the best climber of the party, and years of practice, probably augmented by special natural ability, should give him the responsibility and honour of leadership. If a leader has ever been known to fall, the writer would emphatically advise all climbers not to accompany such an one unless he takes an inferior position on the rope.'

Chapter XII

PUBLICATION AND CONTROVERSY

For I have seen so much can come between
the heart of hills and mine:
record and route, rivalry, quick report,
all the cloud screen
of human witness, dictionaried sport.

F IRESIDE conversation at the Pen-y-Pass Hotel was often concerned with what would now be called the 'ethics' of climbing. There were several issues. Were some routes so dangerous as to be unjustifiable? Was the top-roped reconnaissance of a proposed new route contrary to the true spirit of the explorer? Was the use of some kinds of equipment—rubber-soled shoes for example—unfair to the rock? But the question that caused most discussion and generated the greatest heat was that of publication. Should climbers write accounts of their achievements? If the answer to that was 'yes', then how widely should they be published—for the eyes of fellow-climbers only or for the general public? And what should be the tone of the writing?

From the vantage-point of seventy years later, when mountaineering has come to form a minor but established part of the publishing business, it seems strange that such questions should have loomed so large. It was slightly odd even at the time, for many of the early climbers had been attracted to the sport by reading the books of Whymper and Leslie Stephen and Mummery. Almost without exception, they were members of the Climbers' Club or the Alpine Club or both, and both clubs issued regular journals.

It may have been felt that the publication of books and articles about Alpine mountaineering was acceptable because the European Alps were big enough in every way to absorb all the newcomers enlisted to the sport without becoming overcrowded. It might also have been assumed that the costs involved in an Alpine season would keep the numbers within reason and effectively exclude the lower orders. When it came to rock climbing on British cliffs, the matter was entirely different. The mountain areas were few and small. The railway had put them within reach of the industrial masses. Literacy was rapidly on the increase. There was a real danger that the cliffs of Snowdonia and the Lake District, treasured for their savage solitude, might become—as indeed they have—uncomfortably cluttered at holiday times. To men who enjoyed climbing for the sense of freedom and remoteness from everyday life this was a serious consideration.

There were other, complementary fears as well. If guide-books to the climbing routes on British crags were made generally available, would they not destroy or at least undermine two vital elements in the make-up of the complete mountaineer—his skill in route-finding and his urge to explore the unknown? And if books of climbing narrative were to be widely circulated, treating the sport like some rattling adventure yarn by G. A. Henty, would not the very spirit of the young sport be blighted? The pioneer climbers were jealous of the special nature of their pastime, and when one considers how all sports have developed in the twentieth century under the impact of commercialization and nationalism and intense competitiveness—abetted by relentless publicity—it is hard to avoid the conclusion that they may have been right.

Certainly, the impulse to secrecy in the early days was a powerful one. Some of the pioneer climbers would give, on principle, no account at all of their achievements; this would have been a longer and more accurate book had they done so. One of the Hopkinson brothers, for example, who made a number of early first ascents in the Lake District, wrote many years later: 'To the best of my belief I have never written a word, not even in the old visitors' book at Wasdale, on any climb in the Lake District.' Others believed that a brief factual paragraph in the hotel book, for fellow-enthusiasts only, was as much as was permissible. Archer Thomson, in the first years of his explorations, contented himself with the tersest notes. And when the route was considered dangerous as well as difficult, they were even more chary of giving it publicity. Godfrey Solly and his companions on the first ascent of Eagle's Nest Ridge Direct on Great Gable were so impressed by the severity of what they had done that they discussed, on their way down to the Wastwater Hotel, whether to mention it to anyone at all: 'Where one climber can go, another can follow, but we agreed that the margin of safety was so narrow that we did not wish anyone to follow in ignorance of the difficulties. We therefore left our advice on record that no-one should climb it unless he had previously reconnoitred it with a rope from above.' And the year after the tragedy on Scafell, Cecil Slingsby told the annual dinner of the Climber's Club: 'Some climbs are made regarding which prudence should dictate the omission of any detailed description in print. . . . The man who wilfully under-rates the difficulty, and perhaps the danger, of any particular climb, commits a much greater fault than he who exaggerates them.'

The case against widespread publication was based, then, partly on considerations of safety and partly on concern that the character of the sport as it had evolved in its first decades should not be eroded. There were also elements of elitism and even snobbishness, but these were secondary. It was a strong case and a rational one, but it was doomed to fail. Too many factors were at work to bring the era of near-secrecy to an end—the spreading popularity of the sport, the mounting interest of magazines and newspapers, the advent of club journals and expert mountain photography. The public then, as now, wanted to read about adventure and if it was real-life adventure, so much the better. Books about exploration—desert travellers in Arabia and missionaries in tropical Africa, small-boat navigators and Polar explorers and mountaineers in the Alps and further afield—were already popular. It was inevitable that books about this new field of adventure so much nearer home should appear, and inevitable too, perhaps, that it should be the Lakeland men, with their more practical and democratic approach, who would lead the way.

Haskett-Smith produced two little volumes in the mid-1890s under the general title *Climbing in the British Isles*, the first dealing with England and the second with Wales and Ireland. They were brief and factual and offered the reader little more than an alphabetical account of the climbing grounds available, with information about their history and lore and details of first ascents. They were deliberately unexciting and totally unexceptionable.

O. G. Jones suffered from no mystical inhibitions about rock climbing. He enjoyed it; he knew it did him good; and he believed everyone would be the better for doing it. His only book, *Rock Climbing in the English Lake District*, published in 1897, was the first attempt to portray what it is like to climb on British cliffs, and it is still one of the best.

It deals with the crags of the Lake District one by one, describing the climbers' routes on them with something of the history of their first explorations and vivid accounts of his own experiences on them. The narrative is full and fast and continuously lively. Jones' style is unashamedly personal and the book contains many passages which still ring, eighty years on, with the authentic note. Here he is, for example, on the first pitch of a new route in Deep Ghyll:

> Think of a foothold; double it. Put your whole weight on to it as you straighten out. Take away the hold you thought of, and you will find yourself in a position to repeat the process. In some such vague way are very bad bits climbed, and while gasping for breath at the top the climber usually feels that it was the worst place he has ever been in.

And here he describes part of Collier's Climb, also on Scafell:

> . . . the situation was certainly a trying one, for a downward gaze could only take in the rib of rock immediately below and the distant screes 200 feet beyond. I flung some loose stones far out into space, and could only just hear a faint clatter as they touched the scree. Now was the time to appreciate the joy of climbing, in perfect health, with perfect weather, and in a difficult place without danger, and I

secretly laughed as I called to the others that the outlook was terribly bad and that our enterprise must be given up. But they also laughed, and told me to go higher and change my mind, for they knew by the tone that my temper was unruffled. A few feet more and I drew up to the platform.

Jones wanted to convey his delight in climbing to the general reader and his book succeeds admirably, through the liveliness and vividness of his prose and the quality of the accompanying photographs. The photographers, of course, were the Abraham brothers. He introduced them to hard rock climbing in 1896, partly because he needed skilled support for the routes of increasing severity he was starting to tackle and also because he wanted to enlist their expertise with the camera for the book he was planning. In both respects, the move was entirely successful.

Their visits to Cader Idris and the Ogwen valley in 1897 and 1899 were inspired by Jones' plans for a second volume, which would deal with climbing in Snowdonia in exactly the same way as the first volume had covered the Lake District. Jones made detailed notes about their exploits; the Abrahams took many pictures with their sturdy whole-plate Underwood camera. When Jones was killed in the Alps, the brothers—who admired him almost to the point of hero-worship and who shared his attitude towards publication—felt they owed it to his memory to complete the book. This was the practical reason for their further forays into North Wales in the early years of the twentieth century.

They were not always welcomed by the Pen-y-Gwryd regulars, and the chief reason for this was the knowledge that they were preparing a book about climbing in North Wales. Some disapproved of this outright—on first principles. Some believed it could only bode ill for the sport if men were beginning to make money out of it. Many feared, perhaps, that the Abraham brothers were not the men to treat the subject in the proper, Snowdonia spirit.

The brothers, however, were not deterred. Their book, *Rock Climbing in North Wales*, was published in 1906, a longer book than Jones' but exactly similar in format and method. Neither of the brothers had

Jones' sprightly command of the language but they emulated his manner with enough skill to make the book readable and informative.

It was not reviewed in *The Climbers' Club Journal*. Whether this was through distaste or a gentlemanly reluctance to condemn what they could not bring themselves to praise or merely due, as was claimed, to editorial 'inadvertence' is not clear. What is certain is that one passage in the book led to unpleasantness at the next annual general meeting of the Club.

The incident was cloaked in a good deal of decent obscurity. The sole reference to it in contemporary accounts comes in a single paragraph in the Club Journal of March 1907. In the course of a report of the annual meeting, which had taken place the previous month, the anonymous writer says:

> Mr. Eckenstein proposed the resolution standing in his name, which was seconded by Mr. Rudolf Cyriax. After a discussion in which many members took part, Mr. Ashley Abraham expressed regret on the part of his brother and himself that what they had published had caused offence to Mr. Eckenstein, and the President eventually appealed to Mr. Eckenstein, in the interests of good feeling, to withdraw his resolution, which was finally done. An amendment put by Mr. H. V. Reade, and seconded by Mr. G. Winthrop Young, 'That this meeting approves of the action which has been taken by the committee in this matter' was therefore not put to the vote.

The terms of the Eckenstein resolution are not given and there are no further details about the debate. Nor is there any indication of the nature of the action the Committee was proposing. The only other evidence as to what happened was provided by R. L. G. Irving in the pages of the *Alpine Club Journal* half a century later:

Eckenstein was the principal subject of a notice I received of a meeting of the Climbers' Club (H. V. Reade helped to secure its cancellation) to decide whether Mr. O. E.'s leg had or had not trembled on one of the holds of the steep pitch of Twll Du. As a result of that notice, a tremor of the leg caused by a too prolonged and strained retention of a toe-hold was commonly referred to in my parties as 'an eckenstein'.

So the offence was caused, clearly, by the passage—quoted in full in Chapter VI—in which George Abraham describes their abortive attempt on Devil's Kitchen in April 1897. The account makes it plain that conditions were bad, the rock slimy and unreliable, and also that when George took over from Eckenstein he also failed to climb the pitch. Other references to Eckenstein in the book are unfailingly complimentary, speaking of him as 'a great mountaineer' and a scarcely rivalled expert on the West Buttress of Lliwedd. To readers grown acustomed to the way climbers have written about each other in the later decades of this century, the provocation must seem so negligible as to be almost non-existent. The incident reveals more about Eckenstein's prickly sensitivity than anything else.

Despite Ashley Abraham's apology and the withdrawal of the resolution some ill-feeling persisted though the evidence of it is scattered and obscure. Reviews of George's subsequent books in *The Climbers' Club Journal* were far from flattering. The pages of the Pen-y-Pass book are enlivened by caustic remarks, usually by Eckenstein and his friends, pointing out inaccuracies or misleading statements in the Abrahams' North Wales book. And at the foot of one page in the hotel book, which gives accounts of new routes on Lliwedd by Mallory and H. V. Reade, a scrawled pencil line—presumably Cumbrian—states, 'The Welsh forwards are pressing.'

There was no way to stop the publication of books about climbing. It was inevitable, as the number of climbers increased and public interest grew, that more would be published. The more pragmatic of the Snowdonia men saw this and adopted the sensible course of action. Geoffrey Young later wrote:

> Climbing information, superficial, sometimes inaccurate, and written or reported from the standpoint of climbers of varying efficiency, was threatening to mislead our growing numbers of novices more than leaving them to their own devices and discoveries could have done. Since it was impossible to check the circulation of such information, the only safe course seemed to be to issue a corrective and corrected minimum. It was an unsympathetic decision to have to make. Most of us, of the class of general mountaineers, were alive

already to the dangers of detailed guide books. In Wales especially, among the more localised climbers such as J. M. A. Thomson and his friends, a tradition of almost romantic reticence had already been established. The mystery of the cliffs should, in their view, be preserved, so that others might enjoy their discovery equally. The clearer the description written of them, the more complete must be the disappearance of the fun of finding and of the mountaineering value of working out one's own route. It was only when they became convinced, like us, that we could no longer check the distribution of information, much of it misleading, that they became prepared to accept the only alternative left.

It was Geoffrey Young who inspired and engineered the production of the first climbers' guide-books for British crags. A note in his private diary for autumn 1907 says: 'Started my scheme at Climbers' Club for combining English club journals and producing local guides to stop these terrible accidents.' What he had in mind was something along the lines of the guide-books produced by Conway and Coolidge for Alpine mountaineers. The books would be issued under the aegis of the Climbers' Club. The obvious cliff to start with was Lliwedd. The obvious man to write it was Archer Thomson. The problem was getting him to do it.

Thirty years later Young remembered: 'I had first to persuade J.M.A.T. to break his rule of cryptic brevity (e.g. "The Grey Gully was climbed on such a day"—and no indications!) and to write the accounts of the climbs; for he alone was conversant with all that had been done and could describe it in terms of a common standard.'

Persuading Archer Thomson was not easy. He had, it is true, taken to writing brief accounts of his new routes in the hotel books and longer descriptions of some of them for *The Climbers' Club Journal*. But the idea of a permanent guide-book, in hard covers, generally available, was inimical to all his deepest instincts. Finally, however, he was convinced that since the job had to be done by someone, it was best that it should be done by one who knew what he was writing about. Late in 1908 Young wrote in his diary: 'My plan for local hill guide books to check these accidents by information adopted by the Climbers' Club.

First to appear on Lliwedd shortly.' It was published the following year.

In the preparation of the book, certain principles had to be established. It had to be small enough to slip into a climber's pocket and sturdy enough to withstand the bruising and weathering it would suffer there. It had to be concise and clear and impeccably accurate. A key question was whether the climbs described should also be arbitrarily graded according to their difficulty. In their book, the Abraham brothers had followed O. G. Jones' example and provided a list of the existing climbs, dividing them into four grades: 'Easy Courses', including such routes as the Crib Goch ridge and the Nor' Nor' Gully on Tryfan; 'Moderate Courses', which embraced the Ordinary Route on Idwal Slabs and the Parson's Nose; 'Difficult Courses' which covered most of the climbs on Lliwedd and routes like Amphitheatre Buttress on Craig yr Ysfa; and 'Exceptionally Severe Courses'—the Abrahams listed thirteen of these, among them Devil's Kitchen and Devil's Staircase, Monolith Crack and Slanting Gully on Lliwedd, the Great Gully on Craig yr Ysfa and Hawk's Nest Ridge on Glyder Fach. Geoffrey Young was opposed to such grading. 'I held and still hold,' he wrote long afterwards, 'that such lists are pernicious. They can rarely be true for more than a single climber; they reverse the natural mountaineering order in which climbs should be sought out and attempted; and they set a premium upon 'stunting' and competitive climbing . . . such a list induces ambitious young climbers from the first to neglect the natural and sculptural lines up cliffs, the ridges and great gullies and rifts first seen and historically first climbed, in favour of sensational or arbitrary variants.' Instead of firm grading, then, it was decided to preface each account of a climb with a brief paragraph indicating its nature and the length of rope required by the leader.

The title page of *The Climbs on Lliwedd* names two authors, Archer Thomson and A. W. Andrews. Andrews contributed a short essay on the geography and geology of the cliff as well as several photographs. But the style makes it clear that the book was the work of Archer Thomson. More than half the thirty-four routes described were routes of his own devising. He does not, of course, write in the first person but his mastery of the subject and his individual attitude shines through the narrative. 'The object of this little book,' he wrote, 'is to enable many to participate in pleasures known to few.' To this end, he occasionally revealed his own feelings with uncharacteristic warmth. In the Introduction he wrote:

> ... whatever be the line of ascent, a true mountaineer can rejoice in an environment of boldly sculptured crags, and inhale the influences of rare and beautiful mountain scenery. The qualities of the climbs themselves are not the sole source of their charm: the mystery of the unknown is profoundly felt on Lliwedd, and the element of romance in piercing it is enhanced by the glory and the gloom of the mountain. In this combination lies the secret of its spell and the cause of its cult.

Elsewhere, in his account of the Great Chimney, he said:

> After a series of strenuous efforts we land upon the Chimney Shelf where we can revel at ease in that indefinably luxury of feeling that attends the accomplishment of a difficult climb.

It is interesting to compare Thomson's treatment with that of a later Lliwedd guide book, written by Harold Drasdo and published in 1972. Dealing with the Avalanche Route, for example, Drasdo gives it three stars, the top rating for quality, and grades it as 'Very Difficult'—grading was one issue where the views of Geoffrey Young did not prevail. He describes it as 'One of the most enjoyable routes on the cliff. Continuous in interest though not in standard. Exposed. Traditional.' Thomson, in his descriptive preface, says:

> The most exposed climb in England and Wales. Exceedingly difficult but delectable in good weather, indefensible in bad. Best number, two. Ninety feet of rope required. Good balance essential. No aid and little protection can be given to the leader. Only for a thoroughly expert party. Steepness. Absence of grass and gravel. Excellence of rock. Exiguity of holds. Long distance between belays. A succession of breezy situations.

When it comes to the climb itself Drasdo describes the second pitch succinctly: '90 feet. From the right end of the Shelf move up rightward round the rib into a groove. Continue round the next rib, exposed, and work up to the right until the slab eases to give stances.' Thomson's account amounts to a descriptive essay:

When the second man has established himself to his liking the leader climbs over the abrupt corner. The view expected is completely curtained off by a second and subsidiary rib. This rounded, a rudimentary ledge is discernible on the wide expanse of slabs above. The whole distance is about 60 feet, but may seem longer. The climber maintains his equilibrium by grasping the edges of narrow ribs, and finds it expedient to advance with deliberation, 'if slow, yet sure, adhesive to the track.' A few feet above the ledge is a belaying-knob . . . Beginning a few yards west of the knob, the leader ascends the slabs by small, firm holds towards a little ledge plainly visible from the starting-point. Owing to foreshortening the distance is likely to be underestimated, and the climber, as he works steadily upwards, begins to speculate whether the smoothness of the rocks above or the limits of the rope behind will be the first to bring him to a standstill. Neither does so. He reaches the goal without drawing on his reserves of strength or the last few feet of a 90-foot rope. On this long stretch the climbing is excellent. The accommodation on the ledge, however, is somewhat scanty; neither a sitting nor a standing posture gives the requisite security, but trial of the former has revealed the existence of a singularly sharp spike of rock hidden in a tuft of heather. With feet below and arms upon the ledge the climber can play the rope round the pointed spillikin.

Higher up the cliff, the first pitch of the Red Wall Climb, inspired one of Thomson's more famous passages:

On this part of the wall the formation resembles the surface of a clustered pillar, a succession of rib and furrow. Both are laid under contribution in the course of ascent, for the one supplies niches for the toes, while the balance is preserved by clutching the other. The higher the climber rises, the lower he finds the relief sink. The holds diminish in consequence, and at the height of 60 feet dwindle down to the minimum limit. On the right the recesses of the gully gives a corner to the wall; round its angle one step can be seen, and the existence of others conjectured. By inserting the left toe into a little nick, and then thrusting the right foot over to the notch, it is just possible to bridge the blank interval. For a moment the climber is standing on tiptoe, spread-eagled on the wall. From two slender fins of rock, pressed between the fingers and thumbs, just sufficient purchase is obtained for the transference of the centre of gravity. This done, a fresh difficulty occurs. A high hold can be caressed by the left hand, but a tentative effort proves the impossibility of setting foot on the next notch. It is a necessity of the situation to pay homage to the mountain and 'crook the pregnant hinges of the knee.' This method, indiscriminately belauded in books on climbing, is generally hazardous on difficult slabs. Here, however, the freedom of the next movement is not compromised. The expected holds present themselves, and lead up the remaining 12 feet to the ledge (belay).

The book was issued by the Climbers' Club at a cost of 3s. 6d. to Club members and 5s. to everyone else. It was an immediate success. The chief point of criticism was that it had not been given a waterproof cover. Its publication gave rise to a famous, though anonymous verse:

The climber goeth forth to climb on Lliwedd,
And seeketh him a way where man hath trod;
But which of all the thousand routes he doeth
Is only known to Andrews—and to Thomson!

The following year, 1910, saw the publication of a similar book, Archer Thomson's *Climbing in the Ogwen District*. It is slightly bigger than its predecessor and covers a much bigger climbing area, more than seventy routes on the Glyders and Tryfan, the Carnedds and adjacent crags.

Its Introduction is a particular delight, redolent of the author's interest in the legends and language and history of the region and alive with his spirit, cooly rational most of the time, occasionally romantic.

He was still, in part, a reluctant writer. He speaks of '. . . the attractive theory that first ascents should not be recorded prominently, in order that several parties in succession might reap the fruits of victory with the bloom intact.' He argues the claims of rock climbing as a sport in its own, separate right, not merely as training for Alpine expeditions. He acknowledges the dangers and adds: 'A judicious estimate and clear statement of the qualities of each climb, and the exclusion of any whose exploitation by *lowering methods* would impose on a second party a harder task than faced the first—these seem to the writer to afford the most effective and the most needed protection. There is safety as well as dignity in truth.' The punning reference to 'lowering methods' reveals that he held to his disapproval of top-roped reconnaissance of forbidding pitches.

Reasons of space required that the individual descriptions should be, on the whole, briefer than those in the Lliwedd book. But Thomson still found opportunity for some vivid narrative. Here he is, for example, on the Cave Pitch in the Great Gully of Craig yr Ysfa:

The threshold is flanked on either side by a chimney; each of the two is a stiff problem: loose earth and shingle encumber the exit of that on the left, while the entrance to the other proves an excellent absorbent of spare energy. The cave is spanned by two huge boulders, forming bridges. The further is the easier of access. By utilizing a small foothold on the right wall the climber effects a lodgment upon it, and then reaches its sharp upper edge by a struggle, in which he comes near to defying all the laws of anatomy. A novel expedient is to lay the palm of the right hand on the block, and using the arm as a pivot, perform a pirouette to the south; the climber thus lands in a sitting posture, with one leg thrust upwards to the roof to maintain the equilibrium. To describe a movement of the body many words are required; but this device, seemingly complicated, is in execution simple and innocent. Any Gallio, however, will complacently demand a shoulder. A bastard hand-traverse is now made to a ledge of rock on the left wall. Even without a veneer of ice this is apt at times to be very slippery, and care is required on the part of each climber in turn to avoid a titubant mode of progression, as he crosses to the outer bridge, where a narrow aperture provides an exit. Above the cave a low pitch is surmounted by means of a good hold, hard to reach, on the right side. This is the last obstacle. In quality of pitch and in beauty of setting this gully is unequalled in England or Wales.

Thomson's idiosyncratic style, self-consciously literary and occa-sionally eccentric—one passage, he says, may 'be made *à cheval* but carking care will sit at the horseman's back'—did not always suit more down-to-earth tastes. But taken overall, his two guide books were an immense contribution to the growth of rock climbing and set an exam-ple—in format and shape, in reliability and readability—that has made its guide-books one of the ancillary ornaments of the sport.

More were planned. Mallory and Ralph Todhunter set to work on the uncharted cliffs of Snowdon and beyond, and Siegfried Hereford was asked to deal with Scafell Crag in the Lake District. But the War came before the books were ready.

Geoffrey Young had been more than the moving spirit in all this. He had also been busy checking and revising the manuscripts and cor-recting the proofs. By now, though, he was contemplating a book of his own. It was to be an ambitious undertaking, nothing less than an at-tempt to make 'the statement of the principles which underlie all cor-rect climbing motions, which have been steadily emerging during 50 years of practical mountaineering.' The idea was not entirely new. At the Climbers' Club annual general meeting in 1906, A. W. Andrews had spoken of the need for a book on climbing techniques: 'There is a great deal of useful theory that might be laid down, and some day we shall do our duty by putting all this information together.' Young was clearly the best man for the task, intelligent, articulate, analytical about his climbing, a leading exponent of British crags and Alpine peaks, and in closer and more constant touch than anyone else with the whole mountaineering scene. Even for someone so well qualified, however, the undertaking was formidable—a labour of love, perhaps, but with the emphasis very much on the labour. In the halcyon days of his climb-ing, in the years up to 1914, he worked hard on it. As each chapter was drafted he would read it to his friends at Pen-y-Pass in the evenings, discuss the questions with them, listen to their ideas, and put his theories to the test on the cliffs.

The work was virtually complete by 1914, but the War intervened and it was not until 1920 that it was published under the title *Mountain Craft*. It is a long, detailed and impressive work, dealing with every conceivable aspect of the sport, discussing and distilling the accumulated experience of mountaineers, and laying down a series of basic principles whose good sense and clarity make the book a definitive study. The prose is assured and elegant, even when he is dealing with the most complicated technical questions. If little of Young's romantic passion for mountains shows through, this is because it is a handbook, dealing with practicalities both physical and psychological. Nothing remotely comparable—for depth of analysis or comprehensiveness of coverage—had been attempted before, or has been achieved since.

Chapter XIII

THE DEATHS OF FRIENDS

. . . and looked intent upon the face
of our rude comrade death.

O NE kind of publicity was universally condemned by the climbers—the ignorant and sensational articles that occasionally appeared in the popular press, usually in the wake of some fatal accident.

Although Snowdonia suffered no single disaster on the scale of the Scafell tragedy of 1903, its average death rate was slightly higher than that in the Lake District. The reason is hard to pin-point. There was probably more climbing going on in North Wales at this time, but the new routes that were being made in the Lake District were rather more difficult and the safety techniques employed there were, if anything, rather more perfunctory. In one of his books, *Alpine Heights and British Crags*, George Abraham cast around for an explanation:

My late friend O. Glynne Jones held the opinion that the long, steady, uphill walk was the finest preparation for a stiff rock climb. It was the best disperser of the lack of muscular suppleness which is so evident at the beginning of a climbing holiday, the most sure promoter of that quick control of brain over body that tends to safety when the crucial moment for downward or upward movement arrives. Undoubtedly the nearness of many of the most difficult Welsh climbs and the hurrying methods of approach have been responsible for several accidents. In fact the latter feature, as well as the dangerously loose and unsuitable structure of much of the rock, and the preponderance of vegetation, must be considered the principal causes of the numerous accidents for which North Wales has become so terribly notorious.

In the early years there had been several scattered accidents in Snowdonia, some of them fatal but none of them affecting prominent climbers. Then in two cruel years, 1910 and 1912, the sport suffered a series of hammer blows.

On Good Friday, 1910, Donald Robertson and four others left Pen-y-Pass to attempt the Eastern Gully of Glyder Fach. It was the first day of Robertson's holiday but the route was well within his normal powers and he decided to lead the first rope. The account in *The Climbers' Club Journal* says:

He elected to ascend the left-hand side of the precipitous slab. . . . Some 25 feet up, the climbing grew clearly very severe, and he made some apology for keeping the others waiting, saying that his fingers were out of practice on this his first day. After this for some ten feet he forced his way inch by inch in silence, relying, it seemed, principally upon his magnificent strength. . . . He was then seen to get both hands over what appeared from below to be an excellent projecting hold. For a moment he hung feeling with his feet for a foothold; then, after a second's pause, his hands quietly opened, and he dropped silently and without an effort. It is almost certain that the fall was due to momentary suspension of consciousness, induced by the over-taxing of untrained muscle and nerve.

He fell head first to the rocky ground where his companions stood. He was unconscious and two of them ran down to Ogwen for the stretcher. Geoffrey Young heard the news when he was climbing on Tryfan: 'I ran across the cliffs and the Glyder east crags winged by desperate fear.' Someone who saw him remembered him 'running along the tiny path like someone blinded or demented, throwing his scarf back as it blew across his face.' A large party, Humphrey Jones among them, had rushed up from Ogwen and took turns carrying the stretcher down to the road. A car took it on to Bangor Infirmary. It was all in vain. Robertson died, without recovering consciousness, soon after midnight.

Young said his death 'darkened the hills with clouds that never again quite dispersed'. Donald Robertson was thirty but already had the reputation of being the most able man in the Civil Service. Trained in the classics, a master of five languages and widely read in them all, a devotee of classical music, he combined physical and intellectual strength in a tall, athletic frame. 'No one,' wrote Young, 'has ever loved the mountains with a more passionate yet more reasoned devotion. No one in the short century of their appreciation has brought a more subtle power of analysis and of sympathy to the understanding of their mystical inspiration. His death in their midst was the last almost welcome sacrifice in a service to which he had deliberately consecrated the brilliant powers of a brief but very perfect manhood.' He was buried at Bethesda. In his memory a monument was erected at Glansevern and a Trust was founded to take undergraduates to the hills each year.

Three days after Robertson's fall, on Easter Monday, another member of the Climbers' Club and budding Alpinist, Leonard Salt, was killed on Lliwedd. The Locked Book at Pen-y-Gwryd gave a brief account: 'Mr. Salt was leading (the Horned Crag route), when about 250 feet up the climb he passed round a small shoulder out of sight of the rest of the party and shortly afterwards fell. The rope broke a few feet from him.' Death was instantaneous.

The crags claimed one more life that year, that of Anton Stoop. Born in Switzerland, he had come to work for a Manchester shipping firm about the turn of the century. He took naturally to gritstone climbing and became a member of the Rucksack Club. Puttrell said of him: 'To climb with Stoop was an education. One saw a perfect exponent at work, who ascended rocks quickly, neatly and carefully.' And Haskett Smith said he 'had prodigious muscle power—I have seen him go up one edge of a house-gable, over the ridge and down the other side, swinging by his fingers all the way from the edge of the slates.' But all his strength and caution could not save him on Y Garn when a huge block he was relying on—two heavier men had already negotiated it without any sign of danger—suddenly heeled out from the cliff and carried him down helpless.

Stoop's death was sheer bad luck. Robertson's was caused, it seems, by attempting too much on his first day. The cause of Salt's fall will never be known, but the rest of his party was probably saved from a similar fate by the severing of the rope, presumably because he had looped it behind some spike of rock to form a running belay. Their deaths held no clear lesson except that rock climbing was, by its very nature, a dangerous business. This was something they knew already. The club journals of the time are larded with warnings about the attendant dangers of the sport and the need for caution.

In 1903–4 the Climbers' Club installed first-aid equipment at Pen-y-Pass and at Wasdale Head. It included a Furley stretcher with webbing slings and a chest strap, a St John's Ambulance hamper with splints and bandages, and a handbook of instructions. In the Club Journal of 1903, the same issue that carried a report of the Scafell accident, H. V. Reade argued that some climbs were unjustifiable: 'The accounts of some recent exploits at Wasdale Head make one realise very forcibly that even in English rock climbing there are things which ought not to be done'—and among them he numbered Savage Gully on Pillar and C Gully on the Screes. At the next annual general meeting of the Club Haskett Smith spoke of 'a growing practice which should be discouraged—the use, especially by the leader, of inordinate lengths of rope. Do climbers realise how very few feet of clear fall give a man a momentum which is almost impossible to stop?'

Geoffrey Young was deeply affected by the deaths of Easter 1910, especially that of his friend Donald Robertson. In his diary he expressed his grief, then added the words '. . . Page Dickinson spoke of the feeling of brotherhood, which "was like being in heaven". Surely we *are* a wonderful brotherhood. After a few days reasoned myself into quiet happiness . . .'.

The next Easter brought a glittering company to Pen-y-Pass. In August, Young had one of his greatest Alpine seasons. There was another gathering at Pen-y-Pass at Christmas—'the most glorious of all parties'—and they were there again at Easter, 1912. The weather was bad but they managed some climbs and Young was busy planning a summer excursion to the Alps with Hugh Rose Pope and Humphrey Jones.

James Merriman Archer Thomson was fifty-five years old by now but still climbing creatively in North Wales and branching out into other areas: he had formed a liking for Alpine mountaineering ; put up nine new routes in the Cuillin in 1911; and his guide-books had been a success. But on the other sides of his life, the personal and professional, he was under increasing strain. There had always been a strong neurotic streak in him and his withdrawn nature denied him the therapeutic outlets of the extrovert. He took his responsibilities very seriously. He had been headmaster of Llandudno County School, which became the John Bright School in 1907, for sixteen years. He was not married and had, it seems, no close friends, no one to whom he could unburden himself. He had a nervous breakdown in 1908. Four years later, at the end of the summer term of 1912, he had another 'nervous failure'. As soon as the summer holiday started he went to stay at his brother's home at Worcester Park in Surrey, planning to go on from there to the Alps. But one evening, when his brother was out at a dinner, Archer Thomson succumbed to his depression. He drank a bottle of carbolic acid and was dead within two hours. True to his character, he left no message, no explanation. The Coroner's verdict was 'suicide while of unsound mind'. The Coroner remarked that nervous breakdowns appeared to be on the increase, particularly among teachers. 'It is one of the signs of the times,' he said. 'We are all going at express speed.'

In those days suicide was seen more as a matter for shame than for sympathy. Obituary reports in the club journals made no mention of the nature and cause of Thomson's death and referred to it simply as 'sudden', implying heart failure. Subsequent histories have said no more. Even the local press, the *North Wales Chronicle* and the *Llandudno Directory and Visitor*, gave only brief and factual accounts of the inquest and the tersest of tributes, praising him as 'a thorough Christian'. Yet this was the end of the man who had done more than anyone else to develop rock climbing in Snowdonia. Geoffrey Young wrote:

For a number of us the cliffs of Snowdon, and more especially the incomparable precipices of Lliwedd, of which he knew every ledge and cranny, will be haunted, and almost consecrated, by the memory of a figure, solitary and smoking, crouched on some picturesque and inaccessible shelf, or moving with extraordinary lightness of foot among the screes, the grey curls drifting from the Rossetti-like head, or, most characteristically of all, leaning easily outwards, with half his body free, in the middle of some gaunt and holdless slab, his feet and knees attached to the rock on some principle of balance all his own, and gazing upward with a smiling intentness that seemed half critical examination and half remote and contemplative pleasure.

Archer Thomson committed suicide in early August. A week or so later Geoffrey Young was in the Alps with a party of young friends, George Mallory and Hugh Rose Pope, Humphrey Jones and his new wife. At thirty-six, Jones was already launched on a career of the highest promise as a chemist. He was on the staff of the Cambridge University Laboratory and a Fellow of the Royal Society. On 1st August, in Bangor Cathedral, he had married Muriel Edwards, the daughter of the Vicar of Bangor and the first woman to become a Fellow of the University of Wales. The Alpine holiday was their honeymoon.

Young and Jones made a first ascent on the Peuteret Ridge, the Pointe Isolée of the Dames Anglaises. Then Young and his guide Knubel went down to Courmayeur while Jones and his bride stayed at the Gamba Hut for an attempt on the Mont Rouge de Peuteret.

It was a climb well within their capabilities. Jones was an accomplished and experienced mountaineer—the creator of the Paradise Route on Lliwedd, the partner of Archer Thomson in the exploration of the cliffs of Clogwyn y Ddysgl and the Cuillin, the veteran of several Alpine seasons which had included first ascents of the Aiguille Blanche de Peuteret from the west and the Brouillard Ridge. His wife had climbed with him on Welsh rock and Alpine ice. But tragically, on this climb, their guide slipped on comparatively easy but exposed ground and the rope pulled them all to their deaths.

The cause of the accident was clear. The only question that arose was why Jones had not been able to anchor himself firmly enough with his ice axe to halt the fall. Young believed that, in other circumstances, Jones might have saved the day. Two years later he wrote a letter to George Mallory, dissuading him from an Alpine honeymoon:

I saw H.O., one of the coolest and most balanced of minds, distinctly overdoing it. His wife was physically and emotionally overdone those days, not by big climbs. He had to take more care of her; both of them were steeped in the double romance of themselves and the mountains. And the accident came of his over-care for her, his distraction from the single eye of the mountaineer, that he must have, and that he cannot retain, if he is throwing himself into someone else's being, outlook and performance.

A few days after the funeral at Courmayeur, Young, Mallory and Hugh Pope traversed the Tete du Lion and crossed the Col Tournanche to Zermatt, with Mallory leading in his most confident form. Pope thanked Mallory for 'his introduction to the Alps', and Mallory lent him an ice axe for his impending visit to the Pyrenees.

Young returned to England to attend a memorial service for H. O. Jones in Cambridge. As he was leaving the University Church he was handed a telegram which said that Pope had disappeared:

I wired to the great guides Josef Pollinger, Franz Lochmatter and Josef Knubel, to meet me out there. Claude Elliott and Arnold Lunn went on ahead, and I followed, after organising the search. I was warned by those who knew the territory and the little value set upon life there in those days, to offer double the reward for his discovery alive. Hugh had only just arrived at Gavarni and spent his first night there. It was, too, to be my own first sight of the region. A forested, precipitous and broken terrain, in a great semicircle of peaks, the search looked hopeless, unless I could from the outset limit the area by guessing correctly which peak or aspect of a peak would be most likely to have attracted a young solitary mountaineer for his first day's expedition. I concentrated every faculty upon this, and I have never thought harder into another mind, ready to modify my own first impressions by what I knew of his temperament and likings. It had been his first sight of the region, and it was also to be mine: that should help. A study of the map led me to fix first upon the Pic du Midi d'Ossau. The first sight of this peak, from the pass above Gavarni, made me decide, further, that the west face and the north ridge were the two most likely choices. While the local men were dispersed in bands to search through the forested craggy approaches, I sent Pollinger and Lochmatter to cover and ascend the centre of the long rocky west face, while Knubel and I took the north ridge, which instinct told me was the most likely of all.

From the green col at the lower end of the north ridge, we had not ascended far upon the rough slabby edge when Knubel agreed with me that this was just the rock that might entrap a good climber on first contact with it. Because, although on the face the rock was firm and grippable, upon the weathering edge the jagged corners and large points broke off in brittle and surprising fashion. We moved along upon opposite sides of the ridge, searching the rock amphitheatres below us with glasses. Knubel called me over to his western side. Hugh lay some thousand feet or more below us, in the central heart of the gigantic sweep of shadowing northern precipices, upon the slabs where the steeper rock shallowed off before bending over into the green fall of forest. I fired the arranged signal, with a revolver, to call others who might be in hearing among the nearer peaks. Then we climbed down the side wall of the ridge, using as it transpired the open chimney up which Hugh had been climbing to reach our ridge when he fell.

From the photos which were found with him, his route had been much as I had calculated. Attracted by the peak, he had approached under its west face; then contoured, for a line of easy ascent for a solitary climber, across the great north-western face; and then had made for the north ridge, choosing for ascent the one obvious chimney up its side wall. As he swung out at its top—the difficulty was as nothing to his agile strength—one of those treacherous weathered points split off under hand or foot.

Hugh Pope was twenty-two. At Oxford he had taken a degree in Greats and won a tennis Blue. A tall man, with natural balance and great strength and a cheerful, steady temperament, he had established himself in the space of only three years as one of the outstanding climbers. And his article in *Oxford Mountaineering Essays*, published in the year of his death, showed him firmly in the Geoffrey Young tradition:

> But for pleasure unalloyed there is nothing to equal a climb up difficult rock on a fine summer day. Who can describe the exhilaration that comes from the use of muscles responsive to the call, from the sense of mastery and ease in the very face of danger, from the splendid situations and wide outlook? Every faculty is at full stretch. The whole being is stimulated to the intensest appreciation of beauty in all its forms—beauty of life itself and beauty of movement, beauty of height and depth and distance. It must surely have been moments such as these that Stevenson had in mind when he prayed to the Celestial Surgeon:

> > 'Lord, thy most pointed pleasure take
> > And stab my spirit broad awake,'

> Such moments are necessarily few. It is one of the limitations of mortal man that he cannot live for long upon the heights. But always and everywhere the climber is most vividly alive. There are continual appeals to so many sides of his nature that he cannot be indifferent to them all. Now one may come home to him, and now another, but at least he never falls a prey to that most deadly of all soul-diseases—apathy.

Three times in two years Young had to identify the bodies of friends, shattered in mountain falls. He was reluctant to resume the parties at Pen-y-Pass, but many regulars were even more unwilling to see the tradition abandoned so they gathered there again at Easter 1913. Geoffrey's brother Hilton brought Duncan Grant on his motor-bike; George Trevelyan was there and the three Huxley brothers; Nigel and Geoffrey Madan; and Arnold Lunn and Claude Elliott brought their fiancées. George Mallory and a group of his boys from Charterhouse stayed at Quellyn. They did plenty of climbing, on Lliwedd especially, and Young wrote in his diary: 'Physically as strong as ever, and nerve as sound. Too many memories though . . . '

He also noted in his diary: 'A search party for some P-y-G climbers on Easter Monday on Tryfan. Gorgeous night and dawn. Picked out five of my six-footers and got them round and the party off in 2$^1/_4$ hours.' One of the 'six-footers' was Trevenen Huxley.

The Huxley brothers were young and brilliant and disaster-prone. Aldous, the youngest, had been forced to leave Eton by the almost total failure of his eye-sight. In 1914 both Julian and Trevenen suffered nervous breakdowns, which seem, in both cases, to have sprung from the impact of overwork and feelings of sexual guilt on highly sensitive natures. They were together for a while at a nursing home near Godstone in Surrey. Julian recovered first and was staying with the Trevelyans in the Lake District when they heard the news that the Archduke Ferdinand had been assassinated at Sarajevo. A day or two later came more personal news. Trevenen was missing. It was some time before he was found—hanging from a tree in dense woods near the nursing home. He had fallen in love with a housemaid. At that time the class difference between them made marriage unthinkable. In his despair, he committed suicide.

He was the community's last casualty before the First World War intervened to make casualty lists a daily horror for the whole nation.

Chapter XIV

THE WAR AND AFTER

What if I live no more those kingly days?
their night sleeps with me still.
I dream my feet upon the starry ways;
my heart rests in the hill.
I may not grudge the little left undone;
I hold the heights, I keep the dreams I won.

THE gathering at Pen-y-Pass at Easter 1914 was smaller than usual. Young's diary records: 'Party of 25–30. Robert Trevelyan and Robert Graves from Charterhouse with Mallory. Fine weather after Easter. Climbed new route, Solomon on Lliwedd, with Harold Porter. Climbing well still. Jolly party. George Mallory engaged to Ruth Turner.'

Solomon, which is still graded 'Just Severe', was the last pre-War climb on Lliwedd. Young and Porter shared the lead.

The outstanding achievement of the year, however, took place in the Lake District. Siegfried Herford took his responsibilities for the Scafell guide-book seriously. Together with G. S. Sansom he investigated all the hardest routes and then, in devastating form, went on to create some even harder ones. They climbed Botterill's Slab for the first time since its discovery eleven years before, and they made the second ascent, too, of Jones' Route Direct from Lord's Rake. They successfully completed the route, the Direct from Lord's Rake to Hopkinson's Cairn, which was being attempted at the time of the tragedy of 1903. They made a girdle traverse of the crag. Herford was a bold though very careful leader, making increasingly long run-outs of the rope and climbing in stockinged feet when the going grew really serious. Then in April they made what the current guide-book describes as 'probably the biggest single break-through in standard in the history of Lakeland climbing'—the first ascent of Central Buttress, a long route, 475 feet of continuous difficulty and exposure, which is still graded 'Very Severe (Hard)'. They made a thorough reconnaissance, and used all the techniques of combined operation and rope management to overcome the crux pitch, the Great Flake. Sansom's account in the *Fell and Rock Climbing Club Journal* tells how they threaded a rope through a blocked stone in the Flake to protect the leader:

> We decided that combined tactics would be necessary, and accordingly ran a second rope through the loop. Herford tied on one rope and I on the other, whilst Gibson and Holland manipulated the respective ropes. I followed Herford closely up the crack and hung on to the loop whilst he used my shoulders as footholds. Directly he vacated them I climbed three feet higher and hung by my hands from the top of the chockstone, whilst he again employed me as footholds, which are most sorely needed at this point, for the crack is practically holdless and overhangs about 20 degrees. A minute or two of severe struggling and he had reached the top—to the great joy of all members of the party. . . . We were well satisfied with the day's work, but not with the climb, inasmuch as it left 150 feet of the Central Buttress still unclimbed. Two days later, therefore, we set out to explore the upper part of the face.

The route was completed on April 22nd.

George Mallory and Ruth Turner were married on July 29th and Geoffrey Young, who had been in Italy working on the final chapters of *Mountain Craft*, was best man. By this time the shadow of impending war lay across Europe. There was no prospect of an Alpine season, so the Mallorys had a camping honeymoon in Devon and on the Sussex coast, where they were briefly held by the police as suspected German spies.

The war dispersed the community of climbers and decimated it. Herford became a private in the Sportsmen's Battalion of the Royal

Fusiliers and was killed by the explosion of a rifle grenade in France in January 1916. Nigel Madan was commissioned into the King's Own Royal Lancashire Regiment and died at Ypres. Laurence Slingsby won an M.C. on the Somme and was killed by a shell soon after. One of the leading Lake District climbers, Lehmann Oppenheimer, wrote a moving article for *The Climbers' Club Journal* of 1915, discussing whether he should lie about his age—he was forty-seven—and enlist: 'And how many things urged me on: the wish to follow my son's example; the desire to wipe out the ignominy of inheriting a German name; the disgust at doing such unessential work, day after day, as designing mosaics for churches—fiddling while Rome was burning!' The writing of the article settled his doubts and his fate. He became a private in the Artists' Rifles and died of gas poisoning in June 1916. Leslie Shadbolt became a Sub-Lieutenant in the Royal Naval Division and was severely wounded in the arm at Gallipoli in 1915. Harold Porter, a Sapper officer on the Western front, was twice mentioned in Dispatches and was awarded the M.C. Although he was fifty-five when the War broke out, A. W. Andrews fought in France and survived unharmed. Geoffrey Young's brother, Hilton, had an active time as a Naval officer and lost an arm in the Zeebrugge raid.

For George Mallory the early months of the War were an anguished time. Most of his recent pupils were at the front—Robert Graves had enlisted immediately in the Royal Welch Fusiliers—but he was now so valuable at Charterhouse that his headmaster blocked his attempts to join up. It was not until the end of 1915 that he found someone to take his place in the school and got a commission in the Royal Garrison Artillery in time to play his part in the bombardment that heralded the Somme offensive in the summer of 1916.

Geoffrey Young hated the war hysteria that gripped Britain in 1914 and attended the peace meeting in Trafalgar Square, 'the last protest of those who had grown up in the age of civilised peace'. But he could not remain inactive while so many friends were so dangerously involved. At first he was a war correspondent and by amateur enterprise and determination gained a series of scoops on the German advance through Belgium and into Northern France for *The Daily News and*

Leader. Home again in the winter of 1914–15, he learned that a group of Cambridge Quakers were forming a Friends' Ambulance Unit: 'Here was work of danger, all but in the fighting line, for men who wished to die if need be with their contemporaries but not to fight with them.' He joined the Unit, became commander of a mobile force of ambulances and doctors, and was back in Northern France before the winter was out. For his work here and at Ypres later in 1915 he was awarded the Legion d'Honneur by the French government. Among his fellow workers in the Unit were two mountaineering friends whose pre-War injuries made them unacceptable for the armed forces, Claude Elliott who had smashed his knee on Pillar Rock and Arnold Lunn who had badly damaged a leg in a fall on Cader Idris in 1909. They were both fit enough to operate as roving organizers for the Unit on motor-bikes.

When Italy entered the War on the Allied side, Young's unit was transferred to the Isonzo front in the mountain region North of Gorizia where the Italians confronted the Austrians. The terrain was difficult and the fighting often bitter as the Italians struggled in vain to break through the mountain barrier and threaten Austria from the South. The Unit was kept busy, driving the hazardous mountain roads under shell-fire, and in the late summer of 1917, in the battle for Monte San Gabriele, Young was hit and wounded in four places. His old friend, George Trevelyan, Commander of the Unit, brought him down to the dressing station. It was decided to operate. His left leg was amputated above the knee. More than thirty years later, in *Mountains with a Difference*, Young wrote: 'It was certain that I should return to the mountains. They were my best friends; and even when I was knocked out they had remained so. I ought to have been dead in five minutes, said the operating surgeons, with great vein and artery both severed, had not muscle made silk by climbing whipped in round and closed them.' A few weeks after the amputation he wrote to Mallory: 'I am frankly diverted with the prospect of seeing how far I can work up to my old standard of motion, with the aid of a sham leg and my trusty old right! I couldn't, at forty-two, have *bettered* my old hill-going. Now I shall have the immense stimulus of a new start, with every little inch of progress a joy instead of a commonplace. I count on my great-hearts, like you, to share in the fun of the game with me.' Meanwhile, he recovered rapidly enough to play an active part, although on crutches, in organizing the withdrawal of the Unit after the defeat of the Italians at Caporetto.

He returned to London to convalesce and to marry Eleanor Slingsby, then went back to Italy to work for the unit in an administrative and liaison capacity. He was twice awarded the Italian medal for valour, the equivalent of the D.S.O. and bar. For himself, he proclaimed his characteristic reaction to the loss of his leg in one of his most memorable poems:

> I have not lost the magic of long days:
> I live them, dream them still.
> Still am I master of the starry ways,
> and freeman of the hill.
> Shattered my glass, ere half the sands had run—
> I hold the heights, I hold the heights I won.

Despite the disruption of the War, climbing continued to develop in Snowdonia between 1914 and 1918. Some of the old hands were still, occasionally, at work. E. W. Steeple and Guy Barlow, sometimes accompanied by A. H. Doughty, climbed several new routes on Milestone Buttress, the overlapping Rib Route on Tryfan, and in June 1917 opened up a new crag in the Carnedds, Llech Ddu. Mallory had a few days in Wales just before his departure for France, climbed the Black Gates on Clogwyn y Ddysgl, and led Herbert Reade and Conor O'Brien up the Three Pinnacle Face of Lliwedd on the last day of 1915. He wrote to his wife:

We made a new climb on the West Peak of Lliwedd yesterday. My lead: you may imagine if I enjoyed it! There were some very good bits, especially one near the bottom. . . which proved too big a step for H.V.R., who had to take a handhold on the rope (climbing has just enough of competition about it for the leader to enjoy such moments), and also one near the top, where we were confronted by an overhanging wall. Standing away from it was a spillikin of ten feet having an extraordinary sharp edge. To kneel was too painful, and there was nothing at a higher level to pull on, so that to attain a standing position was really difficult; and then came a very stiff struggle to get up the wall—altogether quite exciting.

In August 1915, a party of five, including J. Laycock and Bretland Farmer, climbed the Grey Rib on Clogwyn Pen Llechen.

The important development of the War years, however, took place on the Idwal Slabs and the initiator was a woman. Nothing had been climbed on the Slabs since 1897 when T. K. Rose and C. C. B. Moss ascended the Ordinary Route. Now, on August 14th, 1915, Mrs E. H. Daniell led three men, including I. A. Richards and her brother, R. B. Henderson, up the exposed 450-foot route which is now known as Hope. It was the first rock climb in Britain created by a woman, and initially they named it Minerva because it sprang from feminine skill and prudence.

Mrs Daniell was more widely known under her pen-name, Emily Hilda Young, as a novelist of everyday life in the West Country. She first visited North Wales in 1906, at the age of twenty-six, and soon after was taken on her first climb, on Milestone Buttress. She was never one of the Pen-y-Pass group, preferring to stay at a cottage at Ogwen where she could have a fortnight's holiday, including the rail fare from London and 'endless mutton', for a total of £ 5. Small and delicately built, with a fine sense of balance, she had climbed many of the harder routes of the Ogwen area in the summers just before the War.

The name of her route was changed to Hope in the expectation that some continuation of it might be discovered on the steeper wall above. In April the following year, 1915, D. R. Pye, I. A. Richards and T. Picton, put up two adjoining routes on the Slabs and named them Charity and Faith. It was not until May 1918 that Richards fulfilled the original 'hope' by leading C. F. Holland and Dorothy Pilley up the Original Route on the Holly Tree Wall above the Slabs.

Teaching was still the predominant profession. R. B. Henderson was headmaster of Alleyn's School in Dulwich. C. F. Holland was to become a schoolmaster after the War, in which he won the M.C. and had an arm smashed. H. R. C. Carr, who began his creative climbing career on leave from the trenches, was also to become a headmaster. I. A.

Richards was to be the most academically distinguished of them all, a formative literary critic, a teacher at Cambridge and later at Harvard, a poet, an authority on semantics, and the co-creater of Basic English. He had read Moral Sciences at Magdalene College, Cambridge, from 1911 to 1915, with one year's absence enforced by tuberculosis. In an interview nearly sixty years later, he recalled: 'Then I went away from Cambridge and cultivated other pursuits. . . . I got another attack of my lung trouble, and went up to North Wales to cure it. It seems rather unlikely but I became—for those days, nothing like the standards of today—a rather skilful cragsman. I was fairly good at floating up difficult rocks.' Janet Adam Smith remembered him appearing in Snowdonia 'wearing a green corduroy suit and a Breton tam-o-shanter and accompanied by a fearful nondescript spaniel who could climb rocks too.'

The period of the War saw some technical developments. C. F. Holland was a convert to the use of rubber-soled shoes on rock, even on wet rock where they were widely considered dangerous, and tried to convert his companions. More significantly, these new parties practised careful rope management and, wherever possible, the stationary man anchored himself separately to the rock behind him while controlling the rope to his climbing colleague. Within a few years this became general practice, though some of the veterans—the Abraham brothers, for example, and G. S. Sansom—continued to employ and defend the older methods.

The armistice found Geoffrey Young still in Northern Italy, being nursed by his wife after a second operation on his leg. More than half a century later, she recalled:

We spent the winter 1918-19 in Florence where we stayed with the hospitable Sir Walter Becker . . . we fell really ill with the prevailing 'Spanish 'flu', and were tenderly nursed by Lady Becker. Whilst convalescing on the balcony in the spring sunshine I suddenly said to Geoffrey: 'Let's start the Pen-y-Pass parties again.' 'Oh no,' he said, still under the shadow of the horrible 'flue, 'it's no good—so many are killed, and who is left?' He referred not only to the War but to several mountain casualties, like Donald Robertson, Hugh Pope and

H. O. Jones who had been of his party. But I insisted and said: 'I'll start making a list', and so that is how it happened. And we filled the hotel and shacks and three cottages, to the Owens' delight, and that was the Easter of 1919.

The company included George and Ruth Mallory, Herbert Reade and his wife, Conor O'Brien and his sister Kitty, Harold Porter, Percy Farrar, David Pye and Claude Elliott. It was a moving reunion. For all the inevitable nostalgia and the thoughts of friends they would never see at Pen-y-Pass again, they had a triumphant holiday in perfect weather.

Accompanied by his wife and Elliott and Pye, Mallory created two new routes on Lliwedd, the Bowling Green Buttress which is still graded 'Hard Severe' and the Garter Traverse—so named because it followed a line 200 feet below the Girdle—which is graded 'Just Severe'.

The outstanding success of the holiday was the return of Geoffrey Young to rock climbing. 'A man who loses the whole of one leg,' he wrote, 'loses more than half his activity, because he has lost also the power to balance, the power to run or accelerate, the power to anticipate rightly the next movement—and, with that, all rhythm in his movement.'

He had struggled long and hard and with great ingenuity to devise for himself an artificial leg that would enable him to walk on the hills again and climb. In fact, the walking, downhill especially, proved harder than the climbing. On Easter Day, 1919, they went, as tradition dictated, to Tryfan : 'The Gashed Crag was my first rock climb, and on the same cliffs where as a boy I had seen the first roped party in Wales. After the long months of foot-drag and zigzag up hillsides, it came as a lightening of the spirit to be able to swing lightly upward on arms and hands, and feel again in balance. The final chimney, which is largely for the left foothold, tried its best to be discouraging at the close.' Later that year he climbed in the Lake District and a few years after that he was to return to Alpine mountaineering, but for all the triumph of his achievement much was gone for him—the easy balance, the grace and speed of movement which he admired so much, the thrill of leading and discovering new routes.

Although 1919 found Carr and Lister exploring Clogwyn du'r Arddu, the post-War years were not creative ones in North Wales. Once again the leadership swung to the Lake District where a new generation, led by H. M. Kelly and C. D. Frankland, extended the boundaries of what was possible. In Snowdonia, by contrast, the lively spirit of the years before the War was gone. Many of the leading figures were dead. Too many of those who had survived were maimed or otherwise preoccupied. Mallory himself, although he made strenuous efforts to revitalize the Climbers' Club, was chiefly concerned with the challenge of Mount Everest. Geoffrey Young was concentrating his efforts on his educational work and on refining his artificial leg and recovering his fitness to the point where he might resume Alpine mountaineering. *The Climbers' Club Journal* appeared infrequently and when it did was usually full of reprinted articles from the past and essays in nostalgia and obituary notices.

Oscar Eckenstein died of consumption in April 1921. With characteristic sturdiness of character, he had not found it necessary—as the royal family had done—to change his Germanic name during the War. He worked as a special constable in London, got married—at the age of fifty-eight—early in 1918, built up a formidable collection of books about the Arabist and traveller, Sir Richard Burton, and went to live in the village of Oving near Aylesbury. Percy Farrar went there to see him in 1921 and later reported: 'His lungs had gone, he could only gasp ; but his eye was as clear as ever, as dauntless as it had ever been in disadvantages of race, often of poverty, dying a brave man—wrapped up to the very end in his beloved mountains.' Oddly, there was no tribute to him in *The Climbers' Club Journal*. It was only later that his contribution was remembered in print and then it was in the pages of the Journal of the Alpine Club, the club which Eckenstein had consistently and outspokenly despised.

In 1925 the gentle scholar and wit, A. D. Godley, died in his seventieth year. During the War he had commanded the Oxford Volunteer Training Corps, and after it he helped to revive the University's Mountaineering Club. He became a Vice-President of the Alpine Club in 1924. Punch marked his death with some affectionate verse:

Long, long shall Oxford gratefully recall
  The pen that never held a drop of gall,
The heart that never knew a thought unkind,
  The mournful face that masked a joyous mind.

The same decade saw the deaths of two more stalwarts of Snowdonia climbing. Ralph Todhunter was killed in the Dolomites in July 1925. And Percy Farrar, who had been President of the Alpine Club from 1917 to 1919 and who continued to climb in the Alps each summer until the end, died in February 1929, at the age of seventy-one.

Towards the end of the '20s, Snowdonia climbing revived. This was partly due to a resurgence of the Climbers' Club, largely inspired by Herbert Carr, and the establishment of the Club hut at Helyg in the Nant Ffrancon Pass in 1926. It was W. E. Corlett, one of the earliest pioneers of North Wales climbing and a founder member of the Club, who gave the money for the hut. The other key factor was the incursion of the Manchester climbers of the Rucksack Club who set up their own hut nearby at Tal-y-Braich. The new developments took place on crags which had been virtually untouched by the pioneers. In 1927, Fred Pigott of the Rucksack Club led a party up the formidable East Buttress of Clogwyn d'ur Arddu. The following year Jack Longland of the Climbers' Club joined forces with the Rucksack Club men, Pigott and Morley Wood, to make the first successful assault on the West Buttress. These achievements opened the way for the second great flowering of rock climbing in Snowdonia, with Colin Kirkus at work on 'Cloggy' and John Menlove Edwards opening up the 'Three Cliffs' above the Llanberis Pass—Dinas Cromlech, Carreg Wastad and Clogwyn y Grochan.

The sport, in the Lake District and in Snowdonia, acquired an entirely new dimension. The routes being attempted and overcome were of a length and steepness and severity that had made them unthinkable to the pioneers. But the new men had many advantages, both physical and psychological. They climbed in rubber-soled shoes. They used the rope with greater sense and expertise. They grew skilful at protecting the advance of the leader by slotting stones into cracks and threading the rope behind them and, occasionally, by hammering in pitons.

Most important of all, they had the confidence that came from the knowledge of what had already been achieved on the cliffs. In every sport the new generation explores on from the point reached by its predecessors. And in the case of rock climbing, the veterans were generous with advice and encouragement. Geoffrey Young was at the foot of the West Buttress of 'Cloggy' in 1928 to watch the first ascent of Longland's Climb'. And in 1934, thirty-six years after his first ascent of the Devil's Kitchen, W. R. Reade—at the age of sixty—took part in the first ascent of the Forest Wall on Clogwyn y Bustach.

Mountaineering is a dangerous sport but it is also a healthy one, and those enthusiasts who do not die young tend to survive, it seems, into vigorous old age. Many of the men who created the sport of rock climbing in North Wales in the last few years of the nineteenth century and the years up to the outbreak of the First World War lived to see Britain once again at war with Germany. Several died during the Second World War—Harold Hughes and E. W. Steeple, Conor O'Brien and Roderick Williams and Sir Bretland Farmer. Others—W. R. Reade and Haskett Smith—died within a few months of the ending of the War. A. W. Andrews was playing tennis for Cornwall in the 1920s and thirty years later was running the Climbers' Club hut at Bosigran. He died in 1960 and W. E. Corlett died soon after.

The Abraham brothers, who did more than anyone else to propagate the sport in the first two decades of this century, continued to climb and to spread the word about their sport for many more years. George Abraham brought out several books about British rock climbing and Alpine mountaineering and his new passion, motoring. His brother, Ashley, toured the country, lecturing and showing lantern slides. Their photography business in Keswick flourished and they even turned their hands, briefly, to cinematography and made a film of climbers on Napes Needle and Kern Knotts Crack. Ashley died in 1951and George in the spring of 1965, in his ninety-fourth year.

The 'In Memoriam' columns of the *Alpine Club Journal* for 1974 contain a sad sequence. Harold Porter wrote an obituary notice about Leslie Shadbolt who died in January that year at the age of ninety. He spoke of Shadbolt's enthusiasm for the sea cliffs of Sark 'which he visited almost yearly, and on which he became the acknowledged authority. His novel contribution lay in the elaboration of complete traverses from bay to bay, the success of which depended on exact knowledge of the tides and their vagaries. . . . It was Leslie who invented the "limpet" technique, whereby after a sharp tap a limpet could be relied on to provide a sure foothold for bare toe or rubber shoe.'

A few months later Porter died too, at the age of eighty-seven, and Sir Claude Elliott wrote the obituary notice, praising his formative contribution to New Zealand mountaineering in the 1920s and 30s and remarking on his climbing conservatism: 'He must have been among the last to wear nailed boots when leading up the highly polished footholds of the Eagle's Nest Direct in Wasdale.'

And before the end of the year Claude Elliott himself was dead. After his years as headmaster and then Provost of Eton he had retired to Professor Pigou's old house at Lower Gatesgarth in Buttermere and almost to the end, at the age of eighty-five, he walked daily on the fells around his home.

The summer of the following year saw the death of Sir Arnold Lunn, Elliott's exact contemporary, who had been knighted in 1952 'for services to ski-ing and Anglo-Swiss relations'. He had founded the Oxford University Mountaineering Club and, in 1908, the Alpine Ski Club. He did more than anyone else to create the sport of Alpine ski-ing, inspiring the first modern slalom at Murren, founding the Kandahar Ski Club, and persuading the Olympic Committee to include ski-racing in its events in 1936. He published many books on mountaineering and skiing and, after his conversion to Roman Catholicism, on theology and philosophy too.

The death of George Mallory on Everest in June, 1924, is part of mountaineering history and his life has been thoroughly and sympathetically chronicled in David Robertson's biography. After the War, he returned to Charterhouse to teach English and History and in the summer of 1919 he returned to the Alps, with Porter and Elliott, to find that the long break had improved rather than impaired his mountaineering skill and freshened his perceptions: 'A great mountain is always greater than we know: it has mysteries, surprises, hidden purposes.

One need not go far to learn that Mont Blanc is capable de tout. It has greatness beyond our guessing—genius, if you like—that indefinable something about a mountain to which we know but one response, the spirit of adventure.'

Within two years he was responding to the challenge of a greater mountain, and in a spirit that was rather different, in both character and intensity. He was the father of two girls and a baby son when the offer came, in January 1921, to join an expedition to Mount Everest. Geoffrey Young persuaded him to accept and he spent the next two summers on the northern approaches to the mountain. It was a far cry from his earlier explorations in North Wales and the Alps and the metaphors he used now were sterner than those of symphonic music: '. . . it's an infernal mountain, cold and treacherous. Frankly, the game is not good enough: the risks of getting caught are too great; the margins of strength when men are at great heights is too small. . . . It sounds more like war than sport—and perhaps it is.'

Despite these feelings, vastly intensified when seven porters died in an avalanche in the final stages of the 1922 expedition, Mallory again accepted when he was offered a place in the 1924 expedition: 'I suppose we go to Mount Everest, granted the opportunity, because—in a word—we can't help it. Or, to state the matter rather differently, because we are mountaineers. . . To refuse the adventure is to run the risk of drying up like a pea in its shell. Mountaineers, then, take opportunities to climb mountains because they offer adventure necessary to them.'

On the morning of 8th June Noel Odell looked up, from about 26,000 feet, and saw two tiny black figures high above him 'going strong for the top'. They were Mallory and Sandy Irvine, an Oxford undergraduate. They were never seen again.

In a tribute to his friend, Geoffrey Young described him as 'the magical and adventurous spirit of youth personified. . . Neither time nor his own disregard could age or alter the impression which the presence of his flame-like vitality produced. There are natures whose best expression is movement. Mallory could make no movement that was not in itself beautiful. Inevitably he was a mountaineer, since climbing is the supreme opportunity for perfect motion.'

For Young, such 'perfect motion' was no longer possible but he fought hard against his disability and in 1927 went to the Alps to climb the Riffelhorn, Monte Rosa and the Matterhorn. Other seasons followed, including ascents of the Requin and the Grepon, but in 1935 he had a serious fall and a lucky escape from disaster on the Rothorn:

> It was made clear to me that neither in the mountain nor in myself had the virtue of my mountaineering lain; but only in the relationship which could be created, and constantly renewed between us; and that this, on my side, depended upon the technique of climbing. . . . I had lost the secure technique which greater Alpine mountaineering demanded, and I had become dependent upon sheer effort, and the technique of others. Further, owing to the excessive call I had to make upon physique alone, I could no longer bring the wholeness of myself, observation, thought, apperception, into natural contact with the completeness and complications of great mountains. The right balanced relationship therefore never came into being between us at all; and the confident joy that belonged only to the right relationship could never follow. It resulted that I must be content to match lessened climbing power against hills of quieter inclination, and enjoy the gentler illumination that followed.

He continued to lead a full social and professional life. He became Reader in Comparative Education at London University, and the European consultant in the Humanities to the Rockefeller Foundation. He was a keen disciple of Kurt Hahn, a believer in education for leadership, and one of the founders of the Outward Bound Movement. His contributions to mountaineering were made now through his pen and his persuasive powers in committee. Seven years after the publication of *Mountain Craft*, he gave a vivid and evocative account of the high days of his pre-War climbing in his book *On High Hills*. More volumes of poems were published and countless articles and after the Second World War he brought out two volumes of autobiography—*Mountains with a Difference* which told the story of his climbing career before and after the loss of his leg, and *The Grace of Forgetting* which deals with his life and travels outside climbing and particularly with his experiences with the Friends' Ambulance Unit. He became the 'Grand old Man' of British mountaineering, not always happy with the way the sport was changing—the sharp competitiveness, the engineering involved in 'artificial climbing', the nationalistic rivalries—but always willing to help and encourage young people who wanted to climb for his own original reasons.

On the fiftieth anniversary of the founding of the Climbers' Club he wrote a long poem in celebration. Its opening verse recalled the earliest days:

> Fifty years since. Climbs then were few;
> And far and fierce the cliffs that bred them.
> Then every ridge looked stark and new,
> And giants seemed the men who led them.
> Mountains still frowned with dread and doubt,
> And all grew friends who sought them out.

And the last verse showed that, although his own climbing days were long past, he had not lost faith:

> The depth of feeling mountains brought us
> *Stays true*:—whatever lies before.
> The rule of life that climbing taught us
> *Stays good*:—though 'men should climb no more.
> Let us rejoice, that, in our time,
> Men found the hills, Man learned to climb.

He still went often to Pen-y-Pass and the favourite walk of his later years was 'over the line of small summits between the Llanberis Pass and Crib Goch'. When he died in 1958, after a long and painful illness, his widow Eleanor and his son Jocelin scattered his ashes there.

Four years later Rawson Owen died, after sixty years as landlord of the hotel at Pen-y-Pass, and soon after that the hotel was transformed into a youth hostel. The senior hotel at Pen-y-Gwryd, where the story of Snowdonia exploration started more than a century ago, survives to advertise itself, with justification, as 'the home of British mountaineering'. It was run for more than forty years by Arthur Lockwood, a big bluff Yorkshireman whose great interest was fishing but who added one climb, Lockwood's Chimney on Wenallt, to the catalogue. In 1947 it was taken over by Chris Briggs, another keen fisherman who was awarded the B.E.M. in 1956 for his work in mountain rescue. Together with his wife, he has run the hotel ever since and kept it cheerfully unchanged.

The sport of rock climbing, however, has changed greatly. Its devotees are numbered now in their thousands rather than in dozens. It is no longer the monopoly of men of 'cultivated intellect' and higher education. The romantic spirit that moved the pioneer climbers may be felt today but it is rarely expressed. On summer afternoons when Dinas Cromlech and Clogwyn d'ur Arddu and the Tremadoc cliffs are festooned with ropes the wide crags of Lliwedd may stand unvisited, as quiet and secret-seeming as they were in the days before the first rock climbers came.

SOURCE NOTES AND BIBLIOGRAPHY

The information that went to the making of this book came from a variety of sources:

1. Conversations with Mr Herbert Carr, the late Sir Claude Elliott, Dr Raymond Green and Mrs Eleanor Winthrop Young.
2. Correspondence with Lord Adrian and Mr T. S. Blakeney.
3. The unpublished personal diaries of H. O. Jones and Geoffrey Winthrop Young.
4. Newspapers in the County Archives in Caernarvon, particularly for details of the deaths of J. M. Archer Thomson and H. O. Jones.
5. The hotel books at Pen-y-Gwryd and Pen-y-Pass.
6. Journals of the Climbers' Club, the Alpine Club, the Fell and Rock Climbing Club and the Pinnacle Club. The Climbers' Club Journal was perhaps, the most fruitful field of all.
7. Climbers' guide-books to the North Wales area, issued over the years by the Climbers' Club.
8. And many printed books:

Abraham, Ashley and Abraham, George (1906) *Rock Climbing in North Wales* (G. P. Abraham, Keswick).

Abraham, George (1907) *The Complete Mountaineer* (Methuen, London).

———, (1909) *British Mountain Climbs* (Mills and Boon, London).

———, (1910) *Mountain Adventures at Home and Abroad* (Methuen, London).

———, (1919) *On Alpine Heights and British Crags* (Methuen, London).

Baker, E. A. (1923) *The British Highlands with Rope and Rucksack* (H. F. and G. Witherby, London).

Bell, Quentin (1972) *Virginia Woolf* (Hogarth Press, London).

Benson, Claude E. (1909) *British Mountaineering* (Routledge, London). Borrow, George (1965 reprint) *Wild Wales* (Collins, London).

Carr, H. R. C. and Lister, G. A. (1948) *The Mountains of Snowdonia* (Crosby Lockwood, London).

Clarke, Ronald W. (1953) *The Victorian Mountaineers* (B. T. Batsford, London).

———, (1956) *Six Great Mountaineers* (Hamish Hamilton, London).

———, and Pyatt, Edward C. (1957) *Mountaineering in Britain* (Phoenix House, London).

Crowley, Aleister (1971 reprint) *The Confessions of Aleister Crowley* (Bantam Books).

Graves, Robert (1929) *Goodbye to All That* (Cassell, London).

Harrod, R. F. (1951) *Life of John Maynard Keynes* (Macmillan, London).

Holroyd, Michael (1967) *Lytton Strachey* (Heinemann, London).

Huxley, Julian (1970) *Memories* (Allen and Unwin, London).

James, Ron (1970) *Rock Climbing in Wales* (Constable, London).

Jones, O. G. (1897) *Rock-Climbing in the English Lake District* (Longmans, London).

Kingsley, Charles (1911 reprint) *Two Years Ago* (Cassell, London).

Lunn, Arnold M. (ed.) (1912) *Oxford Mountaineering Essays* (Edward Arnold, London).

O'Brien, Conor (1968 reprint) *Across Three Oceans* (Rupert Hart-Davies, London).

Pilley, Dorothy (1935) *Climbing Days* (Secker and Warburg, London).

Richards, I. A. (1973) *Essays in Honour* (Oxford University Press).

Robertson, David (1969) *George Mallory* (Faber and Faber, London).

Salt, Henry S. (1922 reprint) *On Cambrian and Cumbrian Hills* (C. W. Daniel, London).

Smith, W. P. Haskett (1895) *Climbing in the British Isles: Vol. II* (Longmans, London).

Smythe, Tony. (1966) *Rock Climbers in Action in Snowdonia* (Secker and Warburg, London).

Soper, J., Wilson, Ken and Crew, Peter (1971) *The Black Cliff* (Kaye and Ward).

Thomson, J. M. Archer (1909) *The Climbs on Lliwedd* (Edward Arnold, London).

————, (1910) *Climbing in the Ogwen District* (Edward Arnold, London).

Young, Geoffrey Winthrop (1901) *The Roof-climber's Guide to Trinity* (W. P. Spalding, Cambridge).

————, (1905) *Wall and Roof Climbing* (Spottiswoode, London).

————, (1920) *Mountain Craft* (Methuen, London).

————, (1927) *On High Hills* (Methuen, London).

————, (1936) *Collected Poems* (Methuen, London).

————, (1951) *Mountains with a Difference* (Eyre and Spottiswoode, London).

————, (1953) *The Grace of Forgetting* (Country Life, London).

————, Sutton, Geoffrey and Noyce, Wilfred (1957) *Snowdon Biography* (J. M. Dent, London).